Essay on Creative Imagination
Ribot

The interest [illegible]

vital [illegible]

[illegible] acting

Too high [illegible] er [illegible].

RATIONAL PHILOSOPHY

THE TRUTH OF THOUGHT

OR

MATERIAL LOGIC

A SHORT TREATISE ON THE INITIAL PHILOSOPHY,
THE GROUNDWORK NECESSARY FOR THE
CONSISTENT PURSUIT OF
KNOWLEDGE

BY

WILLIAM POLAND
PROFESSOR OF RATIONAL PHILOSOPHY IN ST. LOUIS UNIVERSITY

SILVER, BURDETT & CO., PUBLISHERS
NEW YORK BOSTON CHICAGO
1896

PREFACE.

THIS volume aims at presenting the testimony of nature and humanity on the reality and reliability of knowledge. Philosophy is scientific knowledge. It is the knowledge of things in their causes. It tries to answer the questions, what? whence? how? why? whither? Now, before applying ourselves to the acquisition of philosophical knowledge, special or general, it is well for us to make some inquiry into the philosophy of knowledge itself. Whilst thus preluding our researches we shall be providing ourselves with a certain mental equipment which we shall find to be invaluable in our future study.

We require for our present purpose no other data than those universal convictions which have ever been found to be absolutely necessary for human existence both congregate and individual; and which are as strong and as well grounded in the forest-dweller as in the academician.

No labor has been spared to make the terminology here used what a philosophical terminology ought to be. Whilst it harmonizes with the terminology that has been consecrated by twenty centuries of usage, from the days of Aristotle and Plato, and whilst representing the most approved terminology of the modern foreign languages; it is, besides, in keeping with the best English terminology—the very earliest. The canons of language make it eminently unlawful that every one who chooses to write on philosophy should be privileged to change the terminology as he pleases. The bewildering vagueness of philosophic thought now so lamentably noticeable amongst us is due to the very great and unjustifiable liberty that has been taken with the meanings of words. Such liberty is not lawful in letters, in chemistry or in commerce. No more should it be countenanced in the highest speculative studies, where everything depends upon the most scrupulous nicety and precision, and where the slightest shades of difference between what are called synonyms may not be overlooked. The absence of such close discrimination may be tolerated in fervid oratory and in the flight of poesy: but not in cold reason. Philosophy is as rigid as mathematics: its terminology should be as rigorously exact.

It might perhaps be subject for remark that the author seldom mentions philosophical writers except when he finds occasion to disagree with them. This he would explain by stating once more that he is writing the philosophy that has been acted upon practically by *all* men from the beginning. To all, then, since their authority is engrossed upon the open scroll of time, let general tribute here be rendered. Particular mention is reserved almost exclusively for certain leaders amongst those who, whilst as careful as the rest of men to live according to their practical good judgment, have, nevertheless, raised the standard of speculative revolt against the common sense of humanity.

CONTENTS.

THE TRUTH OF THOUGHT.

CHAPTER I. THE NAME AND SCOPE IN GENERAL.

A Distinction—Name and Object of the Treatise—The Initial Philosophy—Spirit of the Inquiry.

1. **A Distinction.** In a preceding volume, **The Laws of Thought,** the writer judged it wise to state, by way of preface, that the book was not a psychology. The same remark may well be prefixed, with significance, to the present outline work. This book is not a psychology. Neither, again, is it, even in the most diluted form, a physiology. We cannot insist too strongly upon the determination and characterization of the separate departments of rational philosophy as distinguished from one another, and as divided in their scope from material or experimental sciences which may furnish them with data.

Physiology, as referred to man, is a study of the human body. Its formal object is the fitness of the various parts of the organism for the vital functions exercised in and through the body.

Psychology studies the nature of the human soul, the invisible vital principle; and its varied vital activity, whether as exercised through the organs of the body or as free from direct co-operation of the material organism.

The facts that we shall have to refer to, here and there, belong without doubt to the complete data upon which psychology and physiology are constructed. We need, however, for our purpose, only a few very elementary and patent ones which are the common knowledge-property of all minds. Hence we draw a marked line of distinction all around our present treatise.

Truly, all that the present treatise can legitimately contain within its rigid boundary must be known, at least implicitly, before any other science can be seriously entered upon. Nay, its great, final conclusion we must have in our minds before we begin; otherwise it were folly for us to proceed.

2. Name and Object. The subject we have in hand has been called by various names. It is not seldom called Applied Logic. With what justice this name is given to it, it is not easy to see. For, outside of the Formal Logic, all rational philosophy is Applied Logic, namely, an application of correct methods of thought to special subjects.

It is also called Material Logic. This name is strictly correct. As the Formal Logic was occupied with the form or structure of correct thought, so the Material Logic is occupied with the material that is found, so to say, in that form, or stucture, or mould. It does not discuss the intimate constituent nature of the act of thinking. This discussion belongs to psychology. But it considers the thought in reference to what is thought *about*. It asks what may be the value of those ever changing thought-contents in the way of constituting knowledge. Formal Logic studies only the progress of thought from judgment to judgment in the process of drawing conclusions. But this mere form of argument is of no avail to go forward in knowledge, unless we can accept the matter of the separate judgments as *true*. What is meant by the matter of these judgments being true, makes up the burden of this book. Material Logic, then, discusses the truth of thought. It is concerned with the general question of the content of thought—any thought or train of thought, any idea, judgment, argument—as having a representative value.

Sometimes the treatise is called Critical Logic, because it judges of (examines and passes sentence on) the representative value of thought in general; and because its purpose is to establish the Criterion, that is, the standard, the test, the last court of appeal in determining such value.

3. The Initial Philosophy. A very expressive name for the treatise would be "The Initial Philosophy," because it deals with the rudiments, the very first beginnings of all philosophy, speculative and practical. It is, in sum, but a presentation of the axioms of knowledge. Upon the completeness and correctness of such presentation will depend the extent of the range that shall be conceded as belonging to thought; and the conviction of the value of thought as knowledge.

The value, therefore, of this initial philosophy can not be over estimated. Yet, in direct proportion to its value for human thought and life, is it all the more easy of acquirement. And naturally so. For, because of its very necessity, we are taught it, by nature, at the proper stages of childhood and youth, even as we are taught to inflate the lungs, to seek for food, and to go to sleep.

To the learner, we believe the name, Initial Philosophy, will carry a very definite meaning; and it may commend itself to adepts, as expressing the search for the *initium philosophandi*, that is, the beginning, the first word, the start, the whence of philosophic thought.

4. **Spirit of the Inquiry.** The whole story of this book might be briefly told by any one who could record what nature taught him, in her primary lessons, about knowledge being knowledge.

To some who have spent long years of toil over philosophical speculations, such a record might, perhaps, prove beneficial. For, just as one may be brought, by habit, to grow into a bodily state which abhors the laws of hygiene, courts the poisoned atmosphere, craves for unwholesome food and defies the clamor of the brain for rest; so, too, in matters philosophical one may, under the influence of surroundings and a mistaken view of personal capacity, become filled with a rash spirit of discovery and, spurning the tender guidance of nature as the child flings off the nurse, may set out, over-confident and half-taught, by paths which are not paths (since nature has not trod them), to grope, at length, in a maze from which there is no exit without the kind guide whose services have been rejected.

Our work must be undertaken in a spirit of simplicity and sincerity. Unfounded prejudice and mental conceit can have no place in it. We are not in quest of "views" or "theories," but, now, in the fullness of reason, we ask to have shown to us some of those ways which, in blessed confidence, we traversed with our guide. And, as philosophers already formed, nature's unconscious pupils, we turn, now, with minds stored and developed, and we dare to ask the question—is there a reason why we shall not look upon all this mental store as mythical? And the response which nature gives (*i. e.*, which we ourselves give to ourselves inquiring) is, that were it mythical, nature must, long since, have pronounced it so; else were nature not herself, and we, not ourselves, self thus being resolved into a pure contradiction, an absolute nothing, or into not so much of anything as to be capable of being deluded.

CHAPTER II. THE QUESTION AGAIN STATED.

Subtle Questions—Two Manners of Reply—A Strange Fact—The Older Writers—A Sceptical Tendency—Sources of the Tendency—Matter of the Treatise.

5. **Subtle Questions.** It is due to our inquiry that we hide none of its difficulties. It is only by the repetition of those difficulties that we can keep our minds directed to the solution of our problem. We have, therefore, to ask ourselves, what do we mean by thought in the sense of its constituting knowledge? And is there, indeed, such a thing as knowledge? Can we, really, rely upon thought, as being, at any time, knowledge, in the strict sense—that is, as having an objective value, as being representative of something which is or was or may be, independently of the thought which we possess? Can we possess knowledge in such a way as to rest secure that the content of the thought has an object, a corresponding something which is not the thought itself? In other words, can we have certitude? If so, what is the basis of this certitude? What is the last reason we can give that the thought is, indeed, a knowledge-thought, that its content answers, as representative, in the way of thought, to something which is not the thought? What, in other words, is the Criterion of knowledge, of logical truth?

6. **Two Manners of Reply.** Thought would be uninviting, irksome—sometimes, perhaps, exasperating—

were it never possible for us to confide in it as a truth-teller. Still, we have all made satisfactory, affirmative reply to the above questions. They are all so very primary that every human mind settles them for itself very early in life, altogether unconsciously and with the instinct that impels to self-preservation. But, when we come to philosophize upon them, to argue, we find that they are, indeed, so very primary as to lead us back beyond the processes of deductive demonstration. And, if we are not quick in our analysis, keen-sighted to detect the limits of deduction, open-minded to infer from the uniform conduct of mind the natural starting point of thought—we shall be very prone, with our philosophizing, to go round and round in a circle without ever coming to an end. For, when we have given ourselves a definite reason why we regard any individual thought as tenable, when we are secure that the thought stands for and truly represents something which is not the thought itself, we have here a second thought about the first thought. Here, again the whole question is renewed. This second thought, this second judgment, which declares the first to be knowledge, to be true—is this second thought, this second judgment, true? Is it, verily, knowledge that the first is knowledge? How shall we answer? Must we say that by the very admission of knowledge we involve ourselves in an endless series of questions, or commit ourselves to an indefinite repetition of the same question, "why may I say that I know?" and, thus, as the question may go on forever, that we repudiate in the same breath what we have just admitted? No; we do not thus reject the possibility of a reliable thought. On the contrary, we determine the ultimate, universal standard of the truth of thought, a standard which *verifies itself* and *stops the question.*

7. **A Strange Fact.** It is, indeed, a strange fact that, at this stage of the world's history, when we are in possession of the accumulated experience of the ages, when libraries are teeming with the undoubted record of past ages, when men whom we recognize as intellectual leaders think their time well spent in deciphering relics of civilizations which have left us no chronology, when the principles governing the movements of the forces in matter have been combined to produce the material civilization that is the characteristic mark of this our era, when the age makes so much of facts, calls for facts, facts, facts, and builds the wonderful pyramid of the natural sciences with visible, tangible facts—it is strange enough that, just now, rational philosophy should be called upon by the very philosophers of fact to add to philosophy a new treatise whose purpose would be to uphold that there is such a thing as a fact and that we can know it as a fact.

8. **The Older Writers.** The Older Writers did not deem it necessary to put into rational philosophy a special treatise to expound the fact of knowledge, the possibility and grounds of certitude, and the conscious possession of certified knowledge. Here and there they have touched on these questions and have, indeed, in this way, presented all the maxims of certitude as well as all the principles for the solution of difficulties. They did not think it any more necessary to write special treatises on the fact of knowledge and the

reality of the object of thought than upon the fact of hunger appeased by a real object called food.

9. A Sceptical Tendency. There were, in the schools of ancient Greece, sceptics, doubters, who professed to doubt about everything—even to doubt about their doubt. But, with the wane of those wonderful schools—the market place for every novelty and contradiction in thought which the mind of man could devise—the professional universal doubters disappeared.

Within the last two centuries a doubting disposition has been revived, not indeed under the title of scepticism—for that is a name of reproach—but under various new names which, from different stand-points, are thrown out as challenges to the certification of knowledge. How this should take place in our day, when the intellect of the world is anything but practically sceptical of its own power and of the objective value of its knowledge, would seem to be, as we have said, a paradox beyond hope of resolution.

10. Sources of the Tendency. Still, it is well for us to try to discover some of the circumstances which have tended, at least, to foster the establishment of this incongruous intellectual position. We shall always deal best and most justly with mistakes when we try to acquaint ourselves with the state of affairs in which the mistakes have been made. One disposing circumstance towards the mental attitude we are speaking of has been, no doubt, a method of study that has been very widely pursued in matters philosophical. Philosophy has been very extensively treated during the past forty years as though it were history, a record of opinions. Often, the chief intellectual labor involved has been to determine the process, presuming that there was such process, by which one opinion developed into another. A much worried method of connecting—not always by substantial joints—the external events that make up the annals of the human race, of weaving them together with some supposed thread of hidden causes, thus adding to the interest of plot, has received an unimpeachable name, *the philosophy of history*. But the same method has been applied to the chronicle of the *speculations* of men. Hidden relationships have been imagined to exist between the thoughts of writers who, very probably, would have shuddered at the suspicion of such affinity, and these supposed relationships have been used as links to join together chapters on the *history of philosophy*. Now, seeing the very contradictory statements that have sometimes been made thus to develop one out of another, we can understand how the method, when pursued with more energy than prudence, may readily be accepted by young minds as a very urgent invitation to theoretical scepticism, as a plausible plea for the identification of contradictories, the rejection of certitude. There hovers about the whole process the spirit that is most potent to captivate the attention of man, the story-spirit; and philosophy is made to go ahead in the easy trot of that book which to-day carries nearly all the burden of communication between the minds of men—the novel. Like other things mundane, philosophy is made to respond to the watchword, Evolution. And we must not forget that the sweeping march of physical science, right under our eyes, from the condition of a plaything to that of an indispensable instrument in art, agriculture, commerce, government, exerts over minds a strong predisposing influence to make them more ready to look with favor upon theories of evolution, in whatsoever connection propounded.

Another thing, too, we must make some account of: it is, the very general habit of men to follow a leader. If we take this in connection with what has been said, we shall not wonder at seeing disciples gather around bold and brilliant men who launch new theories. And this, all the more especially, when these theories are in speculative matters and when, though in direct opposition to the needs and deeds of daily life, they can be held with impunity in speech and writing.

Finally, it may be observed, untenable theories gain a more concentrated attention by being couched in an obscure diction which is, of course, necessary to hide the weak points. Obscurity is a prime element of the mysterious. Mystery has its charm. Hence it is not to be wondered at that many should devote themselves to the luxury of a solution.

11. Matter of the Treatise. Possibly, we may be well guided as to the amount of matter to be put into our treatise, if we view the difficulties that have been felt or created by certain writers, who are still given places of honor and who thus have a direct influence on philosophical thought. The manner of treatment, too, arising herefrom may be the better adapted to present needs in the subject under consideration. Not, indeed, that we propose to consume our time in tiresome refutations. But we can, in this way, so direct the affirmative treatment of the subject as to enable the student, in after readings, to note the inexactness or positive error of some views advanced by writers who are even distinguished for their sagacity and are recognized to have been gifted with no ordinary degree of philosophical genius.

CHAPTER III. A CHAPTER OF DISCORD.

Bacon — Hobbes — Locke — Berkeley — Hume — Descartes — Kant — Fichte—Schelling—Hegel—Summary—Comte and Positivism—What have we to Offer—Course Outlined.

12. **Bacon.** In the presentation we are about to make—one which has its inconveniences by reason of the brevity we must consult and by reason of the need we have of bringing our characters into a common field of view—we may open with a noted scholar of the sixteenth century, Lord Bacon, of Verulam, who was born at London in the year 1561, and died at Highgate, England, in 1626. His chief writings, as bearing in a way upon our subject, are a treatise *De Augmentis Scientiarum*, on the advancement of learning, and another entitled *Novum Organum Scientiarum*, a new method in science. These are practically Parts I and II of a great work on Method in the Sciences. Bacon started with what we shall find to be a very true principle, that the data for intellectual action are furnished, primarily, through the senses. He rendered great service to natural science by the stress he laid upon sensible observation and experiment. But he laid so much stress upon it, he pushed the experimental part of induction ("Laws of Thought," No. 125) so far as to seem to drive out deduction from the methods of thought. He appeared to have no regard for analytical principles, without which, indeed, his own in-

ductions would have no value in that very scientific method of which he assumed the championship. He is called the father of induction. Not that he discovered it; for it is a natural process, known even to the child and pursued by every human mind. But he exaggerated. He was wrapped up in his prospective view of what might be accomplished—and, as we see to-day has been accomplished—through observation of material phenomena by the outward senses; and his enthusiasm has borne deleterious fruit in the field of philosophy side by side with the growth of sensible or material experiment which it stimulated. The world has known few minds so versatile and ingenious as that of Francis Bacon. But those who followed him, accepting with dangerous exclusiveness the method of which he was enamored, as sole and absolute in the acquisition of knowledge, ended by rejecting the mental phenomena which are not perceptible by sense, as well as the immediate intuition of analytic or *a priori* principles which is performed without a series of experiments.

13. Hobbes. The first example of what we have been saying is found in the writings of Thomas Hobbes, who was born at Malmesbury, England, in 1588, and died in Derbyshire in 1679. Hobbes was the friend of Bacon, and, like Bacon, used the Latin, the universal scientific language of the day, to bring his writings before the scholars of his time. His chief works are, *Elementa Philosophica de Cive* (The Philosophy of Citizenship), *De Corpore Politico* (On the Body Politic), a treatise on "Human Nature," and "Leviathan, or the Matter, Form and Power of a Commonwealth." Bacon's advice, to observe the phenomena of the material world by means of the senses for the purpose of collecting data, Hobbes perverts into the principle that all perception is sense perception. But sense perceives only matter. Hence, he concludes, we can affirm nothing but matter. He carries this into personal conduct and politics, making good and evil merely the pleasure and pain of sense, and declaring government to be simply a despotism holding in check the purely sensual nature of man. We may observe, in passing, that Hobbes spent twenty years in a controversy endeavoring to show that he had found the quadrature of the circle.

14. Locke. John Locke was born at Wrington, England, in 1632, and died at Oates, in 1704. He was, by education, a physician; by profession, a gentleman. His work, "Essay Concerning the Human Understanding," has been much read, by reason of its straight-forward, business-like utterance, and by reason of the unhesitating manner in which it assumes to lay down a complete classification of our cognitions, and to determine their origin and connection. He is very affirmative; and this has contributed to his popularity. Still, as his philosophical studies were not *wide*, we must, withal, pronounce his isolated Essay as necessarily superficial. His classification of ideas, or objects of ideas, is more strictly in the line of ontology than of a treatise on understanding. From our present standpoint, notwithstanding the apparent clearness of the "Essay," it is difficult to say what is really the mind of the author. For, he adopts a terminology which does not explain itself in the accepted meaning of terms, and he lands himself in a region which to the critic seems, at one time, to be the materialism of Hobbes, recognizing the knowledge of matter, only, and, at another, to favor idealism, admitting the certified knowledge of mind, only. His unqualified use of the word *idea* (which strictly belongs to intellect) when speaking of sense-perception, with no reference to the transformation of sense-perception into intellectual perception, leaves the way wide open to the identification of sense-perception and intellectual perception, with a resultant of sensualism or idealism according to the bias of the reader. All this is attested by the widely different paths pursued by those who have accepted his "Essay" as a basis for their speculations, some denying all knowledge of such a thing as matter, others affirming that we have knowledge of matter, only.

15. Berkeley. George Berkeley was born at Killcrin, Ireland, 1684, and died at Oxford, 1753. He published "A Treatise Concerning the Principles of Human Knowledge," which he popularized in his "Three Dialogues between Hylas and Philonous." Berkeley had studied Locke. Like Locke, Hobbes and Bacon, he was an experimentalist. But he found Locke to be a materialist. Locke had allowed to pass the hypothesis that matter can think. Berkeley justly argued that if this were allowed, we could not affirm the immateriality and perpetuity of the thinking principle in man. For, with the disintegration of the matter there must be an end to the individual. If it be allowed that matter can think, then, as Locke offers no proof to the contrary, it might be inferred that our thinking principle, the substratum of our thoughts, is but matter. This, Berkeley undertook to combat. But how did he do so? By trying to establish that there is no matter, that we can not affirm its existence; and, hence, as something, at least, *is*, as we do exist, that the thinking principle in us, the soul, must be immaterial. Berkeley's intentions were good. He thought he was laying a firm philosophical basis for the existence of revelation. Locke had said that we have no idea of substance except that it is an unknown reality; that we know only qualities. He laid down, that extension and impenetrability—implying bulk, figure, number, etc.—are in bodies, in that unknown reality, material substance. Other qualities, color, sound, taste, odor, beauty, etc., are in ourselves. They are ideas, perceptions, occasioned by we know not what, pertaining to the unknown reality. Here Berkeley began, saying that if there is no ground to affirm an objective reality corresponding to the ideas of color, odor, taste, etc., neither is there any ground to affirm an objective reality corresponding to the ideas of extension and impenetrability. Hence, if we can not affirm the objective existence of qualities, we can not affirm the existence of that unknown reality, material substance, whose existence was postulated by Locke in order to have something in which the primary qualities, extension and impenetrability, might exist. Hence we can not affirm matter in the sense of Locke. Real things, then, for him (Berkeley) are ideas: "I am not for changing things into ideas, but rather ideas into things." He assumed that what we perceive is simply the idea, that this perception is our knowledge, and that we may not make knowledge to consist in ideas being true representations of originals. For, as the supposed originals, he says, are in themselves unknown, it is impossible for us to know how far our ideas resemble them at all. We cannot (could not), therefore, if we insist on knowledge being representative, be sure that we have any real knowledge, since the presumed originals must remain unknown. The result of all which is that we are (would be) thrown by this supposition into the most hopeless and abandoned scepticism. How, then, according to Berkeley, do we get these ideas? That does not matter for our present treatise, but he is satisfied even with the supposition that they may be formed in us directly by the divine mind. He is as confused in his terminology as is Locke. But let us see how another writer has driven his admission into that "most hopeless and abandoned scepticism" which Berkeley in his unmetaphysical gentleness was steering into, when he thought he had left it behind.

16. Hume. David Hume was born in 1711 at Edinburg, where he died in 1776. His chief work touching our present subject is the "Enquiry Concerning Human Understanding," the principles of which are applied in the "Enquiry Concerning the Principles of Morals." He starts from the speculations bequeathed by Berkeley, whom he pronounces to be the best guide to scepticism. He modifies slightly the terminology of Berkeley, as Berkeley had slightly modified the terminology of Locke. Accepting Berkeley's dictum that we can not know material substance or matter, and that we know only our ideas or impressions, he continues that for the same reasons we can not know immaterial substance or soul. For, if we could know it, this knowledge would come only through ideas or impressions, through the states in which we find ourselves of seeing, hearing, feeling, willing, etc. Now these impressions could tell us of substance only in as much as they resembled substance. But not being themselves what we assume to be substance, in fact, being quite different from what we assume as substance, they certainly do not resemble substance, and can supply us with no knowledge of it. Hence, we can know nothing but a succession of ideas or impressions. Is there any reality corresponding to these ideas? We know not. Hence, he concludes, we have always equal reason to affirm any fact or its contradictory; for we can have ideas equally well of both. He will admit the truth of thought about abstract quantity and number, as, that two and two being four, two and two cannot be five. But that any one thing exists, this he will not allow can be known. Hence for all history he says, "commit it then to the flames; for it can contain nothing but sophistry and illusion." Yet he spent much time over his History of England. Was he more consistent than Berkeley, whose declining years were devoted to enhancing the good will of men towards the use of tar-water in therapeutics? Think of curing an ailing body with tar-water when there is no body to ail!

17. Descartes. René Descartes was born at La Haye, France, in 1596; and died at Stockholm, Sweden, in 1650. His chief works, as pertinent to our present inquiry, were "A Treatise on the Correct Method of

Using our Reason and Seeking for Scientific Truth," (in French); and "Meditations on the Fundamental Philosophy" (in Latin). Descartes was a man of naturally transcendent genius. Only the mind of genius can make a *great* mistake, create a following and stir the intellectual world to combat. Bent upon securing a firm basis for knowledge, he put as his foundation the calling in question all that he had previously accepted by reason or authority. He tried to put himself in the state of a universal doubt. What had he, then, to begin with? The fact of the doubt as a mental act of which he was conscious. Upon this doubt the whole superstructure of knowledge is to be reared. Affirming the doubt he has to affirm his own existence, because the doubt is his. As with Bacon all knowledge was to be arrived at by induction; so with Descartes all is to be obtained by deduction. A clear idea, the clearness of an idea is to be the test of the objective value of such idea. He has a clear idea of God; it is the idea of a Being necessarily existing. From this idea he concludes to the existence of God. From the truthfulness of God, bestower of the faculties, he deduces the veracity of our faculties perceiving objective truth.

There is an inconsistency at the beginning of the method of Descartes. For it is precisely the veracity of the mental affirmation that he calls in question; and yet he assumes this veracity in the very affirmation of the doubt.

He also takes a very disastrous assumption as the first principle upon which to build up certified knowledge after he has torn away everything beside the affirmation of his doubt. He says that he affirms his doubt, or thought, or self thinking, because he has a clear and distinct idea of it. Thus, if we are to take him at his word, the basis of his theoretic explanation of the reliability of thought is pure idealism. And, in fact, the very next step is to affirm the existence of God out of his idea of God.

On the whole, the method of Descartes goes around in a circle; if, indeed, we allow it to get out of the doubt and into the circle. For he affirms the validity of the mental act in the perception of the doubt, basing the affirmation on the clear perception of the doubt. Clear and distinct concept or idea, then, he makes the test of objective truth. Forming a clear idea of God, he affirms the existence of God. Finally, on the truthfulness of God, the bestower of the cognitive faculties, he bases the truthfulness of those faculties and hence the truthfulness of that original mental act wherein he was conscious of his thought and his existence, upon which mental act, however, assumed too early in his process as valid, he has built his whole system.

18. Kant. Immanuel Kant was born at Koenigsberg, in Eastern Prussia, 1724. He died in the same town, 1804. He wrote the *Critique of Pure Reason*, *Critique of Practical Reason*, *Introduction to Metaphysics*, *Critique of the Judgment*, etc., etc. Kant was endowed by nature with a high degree of the speculative genius. Bold like Descartes, like Descartes he attacked the problem of knowledge in a novel way. He made a desperate attempt to steer a clear course between the pure deductions of Descartes and the pure sensism of experimentalists. It was particularly a desire to correct the sceptical influence of Hume which drove him to the task. He formulated a theory in which he introduced both the objective perception and the innate idea, intuition and concept, as he calls them. The two combined form knowledge. The idea or concept without some object to apply it to is valueless; and equally valueless is the perception of an object, the intuition, without a concept or idea applied to it. Thus in the intuition of the objects that come under sense, since they are *all* affected by the conditions of space and time, and as space and time can not come under sense perception, and as nevertheless, the objects are known as in space and time, space and time must reside in the sense power as *a priori* "forms" which are applied to and not received from the object. Similarly, for Kant, there exist in the mind *a priori* concepts which do not depend for their existence upon experience, yet which are awakened by the experience of that to which they are to be applied. Such mental forms are cause, substance, unity, plurality, etc. Finally, Kant divides judgments into 1, *Analytical* or *purely a priori*, which express merely the signification of a term, the subject and predicate being identical in their total comprehension, as, *a triangle is a figure formed by three sides enclosed so as to exhibit three interior angles;* 2, judgments purely *à posteriori*, or Synthetic, experiential Synthetic judgments, as he styles them, where the idea of the predicate in no wise enters into the idea of the subject, and the judgment can be formed only by the individual experience of the synthesis, as, *this liquid is green;* 3, judgments which he calls *Synthetic a priori.* These last judgments he calls *synthetic*, because he can not find the idea of the predicate in the subject; and *a priori*, because they are universal and, being once understood, are, without further experience, seen to be universal. Kant's whole theory of knowledge is based upon the explanation of the possibility of the Synthetic *a priori* judgment. For this purpose did he invent those innate concepts or "forms." Such judgments are the following: Five and two are seven; every effect demands a cause. For a brief discussion of these judgments see "Laws of Thought," nn. 54-57.

In regard to all the *a priori* "forms" of Kant and his Synthetic *a priori* judgments this is to be said: they can all be formed and are formed very readily from a very few experiences. The general idea of space is a deduction. The first perception of an extended thing gives an idea of limit. Two or three such perceptions will wake any mind to the deduction of a possible indefinite space. It is the same with the idea of Time. In the unity of our being, consciousness supplies us with the data to deduce the general idea of simultaneity; and memory, that of succession.

Kant was a man of books, not of men. In the eighty years of his life he was never one hundred miles from the town in which he was born and where he died. His life was spent without contact with the rude intellect. He does not recognize the budding and blossoming of knowledge as found in the individual life of every child. There are many deductions which are made very readily and are made very early in life, and which are thus found ready made, and just as habitual as the most elementary first principles, at the time when we arrive at the stage of life where the mind gives itself to philosophic reflection. This Kant did not recognize. His study seems to have been made upon his own mind in a day of maturity when it was already arrived at a point of philosophic development which few minds, indeed, do ever reach, and where he assumed, as innate "forms," certain ideas that he had become possessed of by the process of an unconscious but entirely natural deduction.

19. Fichte. Johann Gottlieb Fichte was born at Rammenau, Upper Silesia, in 1762, and died at Berlin, 1814. His chief work that concerns us, here, is the "Groundwork of the Science of Knowledge." Fichte accepted the Kantian assumption of innate ideas or "forms." But he went further than Kant. He wished to derive all knowledge from the "forms." Kant had allowed two elements in the production of knowledge, the stimulation coming from the object and the form or concept applied by the mind. Fichte wishes to work up everything from a single principle. For his single principle he assumes the act of consciousness, "I am I." Yet this is not any individual act of consciousness, but a general principle of equality as A=A with consciousness attached [*sic* Fichte]. But this implies that "I am not not-I." Thus we have established the distinction between the ego and the non-ego, between self and not-self [*sic*]. But this ego and this non-ego are not any individuals in particular; they are indeterminate, universal. However, they are contradictory, and there cannot be two universal contradictories, for the one destroys the other. Yet there they are, and what are we to do? The very fact of each one must necessarily impose the idea of limitation upon the other. And thus we come to it that I am my own limited self, ego, I; and you become your own limited self, another ego; and the things around us become for us the limited non-ego. I am a part of the not-I, for you; and you are a part of the not-I, for me. But enough of this for our present purpose, which is simply to show the variations that have been executed upon the theme of the "Theory of Knowledge." For my own poor self I can not find or feign within myself any experience of Fichte's proposed solution to the great problem.

20. Schelling. Hegel. F. W. von Schelling was born at Leonberg in 1775, and died in Switzerland, 1854. George W. F. Hegel was born at Stuttgart, in 1770, and died at Berlin in 1831. Schelling and Hegel are sometimes mentioned in connection with the theory of knowledge, but their writings have practically nothing to do with it. They start from Fichte's position. Schelling had been a pupil of Fichte and Hegel began as a disciple of Schelling. Their writings are rather concerned with the ontological order, tending from Fichte's knowledge-theory to pantheism, asserting the identity of all that is, under a new title, the "Philosophy of the Absolute." From Fichte's "thought producing object" Schelling passes on to "object producing thought," and, from this, asserts absolute identity of the ego and the non-ego. Hegel presses on to evolve everything out of thought and to identify even contradictories in what he calls the absolute, which is an idea or thought. Hegel added the finishing touch to Kant's confusion of philosophical terminology. If we have mentioned Schelling and Hegel, it is to show how serious consequences may follow in ontology or metaphysics from the principles which one accepts as underlying the theory of knowledge, and how careful we must be in philosophy to confine ourselves to *discovery*. There is still plenty of room in philosophy for discovery; but we must avoid *invention*. Invention belongs to the romance. In philosophy we do not want merely to find out how things *might be* explained *if* they *were* as we will romantically *suppose* them to be; but we want to know *what we can* of things as they *are*.

21. A Summary. In the above list of writers we have every shade of hesitation, oversight and denial. One will admit no perception but sense-perception. Accordingly, as sense can reach only matter, we must limit our affirmations to matter. Whatever else there may be, we dare not affirm it because sense cannot reach it. Another denies all perception of matter, assuming that we perceive only our ideas and thus cannot affirm the existence of an outside material world. A third, adopting the negations of both the first and second, hesitates to admit any ground for the affirmation of either matter or mind. A fourth, steering between the first and the second and wishing to admit both matter and mind, individual existence and general principles, thinks to gain his end by assuming the existence, in the mind, of a store of innate ideas and judgments, which are drawn upon, as occasion requires, to be attached to certain indefinite perceptions that are waiting to be thus transformed into knowledge. Others, finally, captivated by the simple method of assuming innate ideas to account for knowledge, go on to the length of asserting that innate ideas constitute the root and source, the sum and content of all knowledge.

22. Positivism. We can hardly pass on without some reference to a name which has been used, in our day, to advertise as philosophy what is, in reality, a dogmatic, unfounded denial of all philosophy—the name, "Positivism." The appellation, "Positive Philosophy," was first employed by Auguste Comte (b. Montpellier, 1798; d. Paris, 1857). With it he labeled six volumes, *Cours de Philosophie Positive*, published in 1842. The six volumes gather dust upon the shelves. But the word, "Positive," had a charm about it. Comte, a mathematician, who boldy styles mathematics the basis of all science, starts out by declaring that the human mind, in regard to knowledge, passes through three stages, the theological, the metaphysical and the positive. According to him, the first two stages have been passed and hence religion, as men understand it, and rational philosophy must be regarded as by-gones. Thus we have ceased, if we are fully developed in mind, to ascribe anything to a supreme being or to any reason-discovered, hidden something which can be called *cause;* we are said to have arrived at the highest stage, which is that of *positive science.* This positive science embraces only what can be gotten at immediately and directly by the senses. These facts or phenomena perceived by the senses are classified; and it is this *classification* that constitutes science! There is thus no science except of what can be seen, heard, touched, etc. Even in our classification of facts we may not affirm *cause* and *effect;* we may affirm only what the senses reach, *i. e.*, sensible facts, phenomena, appearances, which are perceived as following one another, or in sequence. So that the very laws of nature will come simply to this: that we have observed a sequence of phenomena in the past; and as for the future, well, we must merely *assert* that what *has* been *will* be, whilst refusing to admit the reason, the reality of cause and effect. (See "Laws of Thought," Nos. 123, 124, 125).

It is these last assumptions of Comte, taken, indeed, from Hume, that are, to-day, styled Positivism, the Positive Philosophy. Narrowing itself down to limits that preclude the dignified labor of thinking, it brands everything outside of itself as insolubly dubious. What an attraction there is here, what inducements of repose for those who are tired of the muddy speculations of idealism! And what bright hope for the materialist! It gives him a new name for his old one of which he has grown ashamed. He can, now, style himself a positivist. Positivism, alone, is science. Positivism alone, is philosophy. And who may not now be a philosopher? I am a chemist, a geologist. I am classifying facts that come under my eyes. Positivism, will I but adopt its name, offers me the title of philosopher. For it is the only philosophy; and I have but to declare myself, to become one of the "only" philosophers. Shall we wonder that in the last twenty-five years the ranks of positivism have been swollen to armies? I have but to repeat tenaciously that I admit nothing but what I perceive directly by my senses, and—I am a philosopher. There is but one thing to be wondered at in this connection. It is, that men, such as J. S. Mill and Herbert Spencer, who had genius enough to immortalize themselves in writing true philosophy, should be so ensnared by the caption, that their works have now to be read with the accompaniment of a glossary of their errors.

Positivism denies the intellectual, immediate perception of what we call *a priori* truths. These are the truths which, upon their presentation, are seen to be universal, if the meaning of the terms be known. Such, for instance, are the following: "The same thing cannot both exist and not exist at the same time;" "Two parallel lines produced will never meet." These principles we are told by the "Positivist" are not evident. If they are known, it is only by repeated experiences of past facts which we generalize *for the past*, and assert *somehow* for the future. Mr. Mill will allow that one person can make the generalization for himself. Mr. Spencer throws himself out of the reach of argument by asserting that the generalization, for the past, has been going on in the experiences of countless ages, and comes to us ready made. We are denied the power of perceiving the universal value of *a priori* principles, and are allowed at most to say that we do not know whether there are any such absolute, universal, invariable truths. Let Mr. Mill speak: "We should probably be able to conceive a round square [!] as easily as a hard square * * * if it were not that, in our uniform experience, at the moment when a thing begins to be round it ceases to be square * * * We can not conceive two and two as five, because an inseparable association compels us to conceive it as four." (Examination of Sir W. Hamilton's Philosophy, second edition, pages 68, 69). Thus, in Positivism, we have really no rational ground for holding that to-morrow our two debts of two dollars each shall not make a sum total of five dollars. This doing away with the possible knowledge of the metaphysical or universal analytical principle sweeps deduction from the process of thought. (See "Laws of Thought," Nos. 55 and 123.) But it also renders induction impossible, for induction requires the admission of at least the principle of causality ("Laws of Thought," Nos. 123, 124). Thus the power of reasoning is explicitly repudiated, and knowledge is left to contain merely a disconnected series of facts perceptible to sense.

23. What have we to offer? To all these "systems" we have to oppose only some very simple teachings of our nature in regard to human thought and action, without denying what is plainly put before us, and without affirming what we have no warrant for. It is well to note that the essentials concerning this question of knowledge enter into the stock of information that is common to human kind. The conviction of the objective value of thought is a necessity of our very existence. If, then, we have mentioned all these theories or systems, which in one way or another stand opposed to the *sum* of the facts which nature presents, it must be kept in mind that these same theories are the respective personal fictions of so many individual thinkers, each one in conflct with all the others, and all of them in conflict with the convictions of the rest of mankind. This double discord is already the strongest presumption against them all—which presumption is enhanced by the acknowledgement that no one of the originators would have deemed it less than folly to give the test to his own theory in the most insignificant matter of practical every day life. We have not mentioned all who have contributed to the discord; but we have named some leaders; and, amongst leaders we have selected for our brief, yet wearisome, and nevertheless important review, those whose "systems" would seem to cover, as has been said, every shade of denial or hesitation in the matter of the reality of knowledge. And we have mentioned these theories, be it again stated, also because many a student, upon espying a theory that is new, startling and shrouded in the mists of an obscure terminology, has deserted his good judgment to run after the novelty. And many there are who will cling to the pursuit because they regard as deep and learned whatsoever they do not understand. They are ever ready to abandon what is evident in favor of what is obscure and unintelligible. It makes them think, they say. Yes, indeed; and it keeps them thinking.

24. Our Course Outlined. We follow a middle course. But it is not a middle course in the sense of being eclectic. It recognizes something with each of the theories in the discord. But it is not made up of selections from them all. It is the original whole of which they are *exaggerated* parts. It is "middle," only because they are wandering departures from it. It is "middle" because it embraces on both sides and still keeps its equilibrium; whilst the "systems," intent upon the view at one side, let go their hold upon the other, and topple over to the right and left upon the course.

We take our stand with mankind at large; with the ablest as well as the humblest minds of peoples past and present. We put ourselves in accord with that magnificent harmony of human consent which has persevered invariable amid all the variations of time, clime, race, education and language; and which, hence, must be based upon the fundamental note of truth entoned by the voice of nature. We do, therefore, recognize, as indubitable, the following:

1. We are aware, each of us, of an individual personality which constitutes for each of us a "self," an "Ego," an "I."

2. Each individual self knows self as distinct from a vast university of things which are not that self.

3. Each self remains constant as a distinct individuality amid the great university of things not self.

4. Through channels belonging to self, that is through what we call external senses, sight, hearing, smell, taste and touch, we come to know of the existence of matter which is not self and of a body or matter which belongs to self.

5. By imagination, imaginative memory, we can hold before us, in picture, what has been perceived

by an outward sense, and this even when the outward sense has been shut off from communication with the outer world of matter. And by this imagination, which is also constructive, we can put before us, in picture, combinations which we fashion from the varied store of memory.

6. By a power which we call mind or intellect we can perceive, as connected with the things that sense perceives, something that cannot be taken in by sense-perception; that is to say, we can generalize. Sense can get at the individual, concrete thing, only: *this triangle*, *this orange*, *that triangle*, *those oranges*, etc. By consideration of the individual, the mind can form an idea, a concept, a notion, *triangle*, *orange*, which does not specify this or that individual, but fits to any individual triangle or orange, and embraces in its application every triangle or orange past, present and future, and even the possible orange that never shall be grown.

7. There are general *a priori* principles ("Laws of Thought," No. 55). These the mind can perceive to be incontrovertible and of universal application, by mere reflection upon the signification of the principles and without going into the applications.

8. The mind can combine various general principles, or individual facts and principles; and, in the combination and comparison of them, it can perceive other facts and principles.

9. All these perceptions constitute knowledge in the strict sense. All have an objective value. Admit knowledge in one case, and you will be forced to admit it in all others. The reason why we admit that self exists,

that this book exists, that two and two make four, is, ultimately, one and the same.

10. Certified knowledge is not a prerogative of the philosopher. It is found in every conscious self. The philosopher applies himself specifically to the consideration of the grounds of certitude. The rest of men, otherwise occupied in acting upon knowledge in which they are secure, meditate less upon the ultimate ground of their security.

And thus we have put an end to this long and wearisome chapter.

CHAPTER IV. CONSCIOUSNESS AND EVIDENCE.

A Plea for Method—Is the Act of Consciousness Simultaneous with Thought?—Memory and Personal Identity—Object of Consciousness—Some Leading Facts—The Ground or Motive for the Declarations of Consciousness—Importance of Evidence.

25. A Plea for Method. We trust we shall not be charged with doing an unwarranted thing in entering upon our subject in a new way. We have chosen to begin with a few remarks on Consciousness. Our reasons for so doing are these:

In the first place, it is inconvenient to assume, at the outset, without a word of explanation, a point which, later on, may be seen to have been so admitted and may, thus, cause confusion, and even give rise to distrust in an inquiring mind. Now, every treatise upon thought must begin by recognizing that we are conscious of the existence of our thought. We must, therefore, accept as facts certain acts which are within us, and which are accepted by consciousness as being within us. Remember that we are, here, speaking solely of that which is within us.

In the second place, when dealing with erroneous theories, it is of great service, for the sake of correcting them gently, to have found some common fact upon which all agree. But it is an absolute necessity with every one who theorizes upon thought, to admit the testimony of his own consciousness declaring to him the *fact of his own thought.* All the strange philosophies of the last three centuries do agree upon the fact of consciousness and upon its testimony to the existence of thought as being a modification of the existing self. And so agreed are they on this as to make its acceptation an absolutely essential condition for not only the philosophy of the value of thought, but also for all philosophizing.

Why should we not, therefore, begin where we shall have all parties in concord? The method will have, besides, a twofold advantage. It will provide the key for the correct reading of much erroneous or incautious writing on the subject of knowledge; and it will offer a way out of labyrinthine problems, to those who have been seeking an exit by wrong roads.

It will not even be necessary, here, to take up the psychological question as to whether consciousness is or is not distinct from any or all of our knowledge powers or faculties. We have simply to recognize that we have the power of knowing ourselves and the fact of our thought. We may, of course, distinguish consciousness as power, act and state, though all go by the one name—consciousness.

When you say "I am conscions of my thought," you imply both a power of self-perception, and an act by which you have perceived yourself to be thinking, and also a condition or state of mind, which may be described as repose in the possession of a given item of knowledge regarding self. We call them all consciousness. The word, from its termination, "ness," does strictly denote only a state; but, by reason of a deficiency of language, we are obliged to use the same word to express the power and the act.

Considering consciousness as a power, there is no reason to distinguish it from intellect, but it specifies the more general term, intellect, as possessing a special capability of directing its cognitive act to self, to the ego, the human personality, which it perceives together with the acts of cognition through which the self, the ego, the human personality may be passing.

26. Is the Act of Consciousness Simultaneous with Thought? This is regarded as a very subtle question by all who have interrogated their own consciousness for an answer. In every act whereby the human person knows, there is, if not an absolutely simultaneous, at least a quasi-simultaneous accompaniment of consciousness whereby the same human person recognizes the cognitive act as belonging to self. When I know, I know that I know. Although this act by which I know that I know may not be very explicit, it is difficult to see how it can be separated in time from each individual act of knowing. Whether it be absolutely simultaneous or not, it is so indescribably close upon the present act of knowledge that it has received the name of direct, or simultaneous, or concomitant consciousness, to distinguish it from the act of consciousness whereby a distinctly past act is recognized as being a past modification of the still present self, such recognition of the past self being correspondingly styled an act of reflex consciousness or of after-consciousness. It matters not what terms we use, provided that we know what we mean by them; and provided, moreover, especially, that those to whom we speak know the meaning we attach to our terms. The terms, direct and reflex, are employed originally to indicate two diverse characters in the act of perception. In the direct perception the faculty goes direct (straight, so to say) to the object, which is not-self. A reflex perception, then, will be one whereby the intellect, in virtue of its peculiar efficiency, reflects (bends back, to use the material expression, since we have no other) upon its own previous act, taking that act as its object for perception and perceiving the same. Thus the consciousness accompanying each act and recognizing it as here and now belonging to self comes to be called direct; and the consciousness accompanying the reflex act and recognizing the prior act perceived as belonging at some distinctly previous time to the present identical self comes to be called reflex. For the sake of a distinction we might, when speaking of consciousness (which brings the self-element into the perception), use the term, simultaneous or concomitant, instead of direct; and we might say continuous consciousness or after-consciousness instead of reflex consciousness.

To guard against misunderstanding, it may be well to note that the expression "reflex act of consciousness" has a wider signification than the expression "reflex act of intellect." In the strict meaning of terms, intellect is said to reflect back upon a prior act of intellect. Consciousness, whatever consciousness may be, goes back to any prior perception, sensitive or intellectual, that may have existed in the totality of the *ego*. This may not be clear just now; but it is well to have the distinction recorded.

27. Memory and Personal Identity. We hold, and we must hold, that the human person is a unit. Self, the ego, the me, is the same self to-day, yesterday, to-morrow. The continuous identity of the same self is manifested to us in the repeated states of consciousness. It is memory, mysterious memory, that links together in knowledge, and thus preserves in consciousness, the identity of self to whom successive acts of self-knowledge and states of consciousness belong.

Memory is the power we possess of laying by knowledge and bringing it up again. It is the power of reviving, so to say, a past state of consciousness. It might be objected to this assertion, that when we remember, we very rarely call to mind a past state of consciousness. True enough, when we remember, we do not always make an explicit consideration of some past state of consciousness. Nevertheless, in every act of memory there is an implicit reference to a past state of consciousness. You may say that you remember things that are altogether outside of consciousness and have no relation to it; as the purchase of Alaska by the United States, an eruption of Mt. Aetna, the first expedition up the Congo. Still, consider what you wish here to signify in saying "I remember." You wish to state that, at a certain time past, you possessed certain items of knowledge regarding what was outside of you and that the knowledge was bound up with a self which was conscious of its knowledge and itself at that time past. You mean, also, that the past conscious self is identical with the present conscious self, and that this identity of self, the human person, is proclaimed by memory. You imply, that, knowledge, possessed by past self, may be revived in present self. Finally, you use the expression, "I remember" and not "I know," for the purpose of indicating the identity of present self and past self, the continuity of consciousness, and the linking by memory of that prior consciousness of knowledge to the present self, conscious of its own past state of conscious knowledge. All this you mean. And this process you go through, implicitly; nay, perhaps, even explicitly;—the process, like all others that are essential to human existence, having become so rapid and spontaneous as to elude observation. At all events, nature puts the whole proceeding into a formula for you: "I remember."

28. **Object of Consciousness.** The object of a faculty is that upon which the faculty exercises itself. The object of consciousness is self, I, the individual human personality, as undergoing some modification of self. These modifications are, first, all cognitions or perceptions; secondly, all modifications with which cognition is intimately connected and necessarily associated. In this way we bring under the object of consciousness all volitions, or acts of will, which are, necessarily, accompanied by thought; as also pain and pleasure, which are perceived as being departures from the normal condition of self: and we exclude such things as the regular circulation of the blood and

the normal bodily temperature, which we do not perceive as modifications or changes of self.

29. Some Leading Facts. Some leading facts reached by consciousness and included in its object, are:

1. The existence of self, of the me, the human person, perceived in every act of consciousness.
2. The fact of thought: that is, judgment, mental assent or denial; ideas, the elements of judgment; and reasoning, the combination of judgments.
3. Certain states of self which consciousness inevitably connects with body-belonging-to-self, and perceives as impossible without that element of body-belonging-to-self. Such are the states called seeing, hearing, smelling, tasting, touching. Consciousness, also, links these states, by inevitable connection, to separate parts, respectively, of the body-belonging-to-self: to eyes, ears, nostrils, tongue and palate, body surface.
4. A twofold representation by idea: the idea sometimes relating to but one individual, and sometimes embracing all the individuals of a class; as, the idea of this man and of man in general.
5. Finally, consciousness testifies to an irrepressible tendency of the conscious self to regard its states, which are states of cognition, as indicative, sometimes, of realities in self and, sometimes, of realities out of self.

30. The Ground or Motive for the Declarations of Consciousness. This is something to be determined very accurately, for upon it must rest the whole of our treatise. Why do I declare, without hesitation, the fact of my thought and of myself? Because I am conscious of it. But what do I mean by saying that I am conscious of it? I mean that I know it. But, how or why do I know it? I know it because being something knowable, and as knowable being within the scope of my knowing power, it is presented to me in such a way as to allow me to exercise my power of knowing upon it—or, more correctly, it is presented to me in such a way that I am forced to exercise my knowing power upon it, that is, to know it. What is there, then, in the fact, in my thought and the existence of self, which constitutes the reason, the ultimate reason, why my knowing power must start into activity, upon the presence of the fact—and know the fact? This something we call the *evidence* of the fact. The fact is evident, visible (mentally), perceptible to me; and my knowing power (consciousness), which acts spontaneously upon the presentation of evident truth, must know it. I must hold to the objective value of the fact or truth so perceived as evident. I hold to it without any fear of error, that is to say, with certitude; and this I do, because it is evident to me. In assigning reasons for my certitude, I cannot go beyond this evidence.

31. Importance of Evidence. Upon the admission of the value of evidence as a motive of certitude, as the final motive, depends the whole question concerning the objective value of knowledge. Admit evidence as a sufficient motive for certitude in the assertion of self and the thoughts and various modifications of self, and you must admit it to be a sufficient motive for affirming with certitude the objective truth of existences and general principles that are neither self nor modifications of self. And if you will not admit evidence to be a sufficient motive for certitude regarding *self* and its modifications, you cannot affirm even your own existence and must therefore be considered to be outside of our audience.

CHAPTER V. THE AFFIRMATION OF AN OBJECT THAT IS NOT SELF.

The Great Question—To be Conscious is to Know—Transit to Non-Self—Example—General Inference.

32. The Great Question. We have seen how all the theorists agree with the common sense, the common judgment of mankind, in admitting the value of the testimony of consciousness for the existence of self and the modifications of self. The great question, now, is: Can we in any way secure a certified conviction of the reality of something that is not self? Consciousness testifies that we do seem, at least, to perceive that which is not self and that we are thus inclined to affirm something that is not self. All the theorists admit this; but they fear to affirm, uniformly, the objective value of these "seemings." Thus we seem to perceive a material world as if it were objectively true, as if it really existed—as really, indeed, as self itself. We seem, also, to perceive certain general principles such as "two and two are four," as if they had an objective value independently of the perception. These are not-self. May we affirm them with the same security with which we affirm self? The answer is, Yes.

33. To be Conscious is to Know. Let us for the time being rid ourselves of the expression, to be conscious, and use its equivalent. To be conscious is to know *self*. It is, then, an act of knowing with this special feature that the object known is self. To be conscious *(conscire)*, then, is nothing more than to know *(scire)*. The special term made up by compounding with the prefix *con*, indicates that the object known is self. And why is self known? Because, being knowable, it comes with its evidence within reach of our knowing power. It is merely a knowable something that *happens* to be self. And I affirm that something, solely because it is evident to me. And I affirm it to be self, because it presents itself to me with its credentials, that is, with its evidence as self.

34. Transit to Non-Self. How, then, can I know and affirm as objectively true, that which is not self? In the very same manner and for the very same reason that I affirm self; that is, because something which is not self, being in itself knowable, presents itself with its evidence to my knowing power to be known; and I am forced to know that which is so presented to me, as I am forced to know myself. And as self is known to be self because it presents itself as self, so not-self is known to be not-self because it presents itself as not-self. So that if we will not affirm non-self upon its evidence, neither have we any right to affirm self upon *its* evidence.

35. Example. Let me be conscious of a thought. I am thinking of a deep, dark sky spangled with brilliant stars. I know the thought as mine. Yes, but the bright lights upon the dark canopy! I open and close my eyes. This action I know, also, as mine. I repeat the opening and closing of my eyes. There appears and disappears and re-appears a brilliant vivid counterpart of my thought. Whilst my eyes are open, it is there; when my eyes are closed, it is gone. This brilliant splendor presents itself to me, not as something which is a modification of me, not as mixed up with the existence of myself; but as a something whose existence is distinct from and independent of myself. I know it as not-self; and I know it as such by the evidence of not-self wherewith it presents itself to me. And just as in the perception or knowing of self I affirm self, so also, for the same reason, evidence, I affirm, with inevitable conviction, the objective value of non-self. I have a thought or a headache. The thought or the headache presents itself to me as mine. I thereupon have a conviction that it is mine. Of this conviction, certified in the perception of what is evident, I can not rid myself; and I hold to it. The midnight glory of the stars presents itself to me as a something which excludes the element of myself. I have, thereupon, a conviction of that something, as strong as the conviction of my own thought; and simultaneously I have a conviction that that something is distinct from me. Of this conviction, certified in the perception of what is evident, I can not rid myself; and I hold to it.

Yes, you may say, but how do you *know* that these external objects *are* at all? I will answer you if you tell me how you know you have a headache. For your headache is, certainly, something distinct from your perceiving power. You will admit the existence of the headache, because perceived with its evidence of being in self. So you must admit the existence of that something which we call the golden glory of the stars, because it is perceived with its evidence of being out of self. If you deny the second you must deny the first, and, thus, put yourself in the bleak region outside the pale of reason.

36. General Inference. What we have just said of vision, applies with strict universality to all the knowing powers, and justifies us in affirming, upon evidence, the objective truth of the world of matter as perceived by sense; of the analytic principle, as reached by the intellect; of self, as reported by consciousness.

In fact, to turn the tables upon our adversaries, we can make it harder for them to explain the affirmation of self than the affirmation of non-self. For, the affirmation of self, of my own thought, requires a reflex action whereby my thinking power turns upon itself; whereas the affirmation of non-self does not demand such reflex action.

CHAPTER VI. SCEPTICISM.

Dogmatic and Non-Dogmatic Scepticism—Partial Scepticism—Inconsistency—A Practical Consideration—An Advantage Gained—The Work Before Us.

37. Dogmatic and Non-Dogmatic Scepticism. It is necessary, for a further advance, to clear the ground of scepticism. We are in position, now, to do so. We can have no hesitation hanging over us. We are looking for the positive in rational philosophy.

There are two kinds of scepticism, dogmatic and non-dogmatic. The dogmatic sceptic holds that the mind is and can be in the state of doubt, only, in regard to all things excepting the fact of the doubt. Of his doubt he claims to be certain; in this he is dogmatic. The non-dogmatic sceptic is not ready to assert even his doubt. If you question him, he will reply that he doubts whether he doubts; and he will doubt, again, whether he doubts that he doubts of his doubt—and so on *ad indefinitum*.

You can have no argument with a non-dogmatic sceptic. For, he will doubt whether you are speaking to him. He will doubt of your existence and of HIS OWN EXISTENCE. You can hope, therefore, to convince him of nothing. Happily, the sceptics of this class have been left behind in ancient Greece; and are, now, spoken of only in amusing stories.

The dogmatic sceptic offers us a starting point for argument. This is his tenet, that he *does* doubt, that he is *sure* of his *doubt* about *all* things, and that he is sure of nothing else. He also gives us a hold when he makes his inconsistent attempt to prove the necessity of his state of doubt. For in affirming his doubt, he affirms his own existence; and in trying to prove his doubt he assumes the objective value of reasoning, of judgments and of ideas.

Dogmatic sceptics, open and avowed, in the universal sense just mentioned, we will hardly meet with.

38. Partial Scepticism. But if we look back to Chapter III, we shall see that it is nothing less than scepticism that is concealed in the writings of Kant, Hume, Descartes, Spencer and others there mentioned; a scepticism adorned with a new name, idealism, materialism, positivism, etc., in all of which there is a professed doubt (if not an open denial) of the objective value of certain acts of cognition. With the very same reason at hand for admitting the objective value of all acts of cognition, these writers admit the evidence in one case, and, very inconsistently, reject it in another. In this sense, then, are they sceptics, and very dogmatic, too.

Hence, the name of sceptic is very justly applicable to any one who rejects the testimony of any of the knowledge-faculties. In practical life, none of the writers referred to were sceptics—neither Kant nor Descartes, nor any of them. Even Hume, called the Father of modern sceptics, avowed that, in practice, he thought and acted as other men. But the mistake which all these writers have made is, that they have tried to explain the fact of knowledge by leaving out one or more of the knowledge-faculties. The idealist tries to explain cognition, without a veritable perception through the senses; all cognition, as such, originating, according to him, purely in intellect. The materialist and positivist, on the other hand, try to explain cognition upon the assumption that all is matter, or that we can rely upon sense perception, only. Hence, they practically deny intellect, reject the perception of *a priori* truths, and discard the intellectual process of deduction.

39. Inconsistency. The whole mistake of the partial sceptic lies in his accepting one knowledge power and rejecting another; in admitting evidence in one case and repudiating it in another. Why, I ask, should he trust to nature's guidance in one instance, and not in another? He puts himself in a very awkward predicament. He can not advance a step without being inconsistent. Facts perceptible by sense, and *a priori* principles perceptible in their universal character, are, both, necessary for argument with men. For, he who will not admit perception by sense, must simply assume without warrant the existence of men like himself, since their existence can be reached by real sense-perception only. And he who will not admit the purely intellectual perception of purely *a priori* truths in their general and universal character which is not perceptible to any sense, deprives himself of the very basis of all argument, of the general objective value of the principle of equality, *i. e.*, that two things which, in a respect, are equal to a third, are, in the same respect, equal to one another. He even deprives himself of the chance of holding to any single judgment. For, to him, there is no absolute value in the principle of contradiction, taken generally, *i. e.*, that the same thing cannot both be and not be at the same time. Hence, he must always be prepared, at the outset of his argument, to affirm and deny the same thing at the same time. In this way, then, is materialism reducible to the most hopeless scepticism. The great argument against the sceptic consists, then, radically, in forcing upon him his inconsistency in admitting one evidence and rejecting another; his inconsistency in trusting one cognitive faculty and doubting the fidelity of another; and his double inconsistency, when he begins to reason, of assuming, in his argument, a cognitive power and an evidence which he has rejected at the start. For, as we have seen, every attempt at argument amongst men demands and assumes the objective value of both sense-perception and intellectual perception; perception of the individual fact of another man's material body by means of sense, and perception of general, universal truths by intellect.

40. A Practical Consideration. No valid argument can be brought forward to discredit the objective value of either sense perception or intellectual perception. Every argument advanced by the whole range of theoretic sceptics, assumes as a certainty the very thing which it wishes to prove uncertain or unknowable. When we take up a book which proposes to manifest to us that we can have no certified conviction of the outer world such as we accept it, what do we find? We find the writer assuming not only the existence of his own intelligence, and of his own body with its various organs, but also the existence of his pen and paper, and of a power of vision to guide him in faithfully transcribing the thought of his intellect. We find him assuming my existence and your existence, my intelligence and your intelligence, my organs of vision and your organs of vision, and the capacity of these organs to transmit, faithfully, the words upon the paper. We find him assuming the reality of the printing press, and we discover him reading the proofs very carefully so as to have the bound volume objectively correct. And when that book comes to him from the publisher, he will turn over its leaves with complacency at the thought of having proved to us that we have no right to affirm it to be what he himself so clearly holds it to be. Now, if this is philosophy, the life of the philosopher is a very idle sort of a dream. Besides, if you eliminate the conviction that any objective verity is what it presents itself with its evidence to be, you, at that moment, make practical life an impossibility. But the philosophy that makes human life an impossibility is not the philosophy for man. Howsoever it might suit certain fictitious existences that we know nothing of, we shall not undertake to inquire; but it does not suit the real human existence, with which, after all, it purports to be occupied. Carried out, it makes that life an impossibility: therefore is it a false philosophy.

In accounting for cognition, it is no more lawful to deny or ignore a knowledge power that evidences itself than it would be to introduce arbitrarily and without any evidence some new kind of a power and to insist upon all men admitting that they possessed such a power whilst each man's consciousness testifies to him that he does not possess it. The one position is as unreasonable as the other. Yet our theoretical sceptics insist upon the one, whilst they would blush at the other.

When a great problem presents itself—like that of the twofold character of knowledge, the knowledge of self and not-self—it is far more manly to face the whole problem and to acknowledge the limitations of our analysis, than to deny the intricacies of the solution, take half of the problem as already solved and on the assumption build up an arbitrary "system" which all men must then call philosophy or be regarded as lacking intelligence. Yet this is the method pursued by every form of theoretic scepticism, call it idealism, phenomenalism, materialism or agnosticism. The theoretic sceptic, nevertheless, in practical life, acts up to his conviction of the objective truth of both facts and principles. He goes to dinner and to bed. He pays and collects his bills. Though he lectures in the university and writes books to prove to you and me that we must not take things as they seem to be, he himself does, all the time, take them to be as they seem to him to be; and he would not for a moment dare to do otherwise. So do Berkeley, Hume, Kant, J. S. Mill, H. Spencer, whilst writing books (which are very hard reading) to show that any one else who should presume to do likewise would be pursuing a course for which reason grants no warrant.

41. An Advantage Gained. The advantage which we hope we have gained by the method of treatment which we have thus far pursued is not an inconsiderable one. We have tried to rid the following pages from a constant warfare which we should, otherwise, find ourselves obliged to keep up with conflicting theories. We are following what may be called, in a sense, the middle course, in as much as we are not dragged over to the extreme of either idealism or sensualism. We are trying to indicate the entire philosophy of the convictions that govern and have ever governed the practical life of men, and which are the essential condition of thought, of civilization, of progress, of human existence. In the pages which are to come we should find it very tedious were we obliged at every paragraph to make a reference to what had been said by one or another of the theorists mentioned in Chapter III, and to indulge in a refutation. To avoid this inconvenience we have massed the opposition into one chapter. In the discord we have found that all the theories are built upon the same foundation, evidence. But the theorists did not take into their field of view the whole foundation, the whole evidence. Each, arbitrarily limiting himself to one particular evidence, to half the foundation (ignoring the other half), and having built thereupon his structure, has no way left him to complete the edifice of knowledge but by building on top of what he already has—a castle in the air. This superstructure has no stability. Thus, for instance, the idealist affirming self upon the evidence of self, tries, out of this affirmation and without evidence, to affirm not-self and the outer world in general, or declares, at least, that there is no other basis upon which to establish the conviction of not-self, if, indeed, we will insist upon having such a conviction. He ignores the other evidences, the other parts of the foundation. He has built a castle in the air. To affirm it to be real is to put upon the partial evidence the whole weight of the entire objective truth, and, in this case, the partial evidence, itself, must crumble, for it is not destined to support the mass; and there is left the chaos of nescience.

We opened upon a common ground, consciousness, for the reason that when dealing with one or another of the multifarious vagaries of philosophic thought upon the question with which we are occupied, we shall always find it more easy to lead an inquirer forward from a common ground than to seek him in every by-way of his wanderings and guide him back constantly to the starting point: besides, when we proffer safe conduct to the meeting of the ways, a wanderer may be ill disposed to submit to our guidance.

42. The Work Before Us. We could not go on with the rest of our work by the pure analysis of inquiry, for we should never come to an end. Recognizing, now, the entire scope of evidence as presenting to us that which is knowable, we are prepared to see what is held regarding the truth of thought by the human race, taught from the beginning in the great University of nature.

CHAPTER VII. THE TRUTH OF THOUGHT, OR LOGICAL TRUTH.

Truth: Ontological, Logical, Moral—Truth, a Certain Correspondence or Conformity—Logical Truth—Logical Falsity—Logical Truth; in what Mental Act is it Found—The Radical Reason.

43. Truth: Ontological, Logical, Moral. If we consider the various uses of the words, *true*, *truth*, we shall find that there are three orders of truth. We say of a man that he is a true orator, meaning that he contains within himself, that he possesses the requisites of an orator; that he corresponds to the ideal which we figure to ourselves as the pattern to which the real must conform to be truly an orator. This correspondence of real with the ideal is called ontological truth. It is the truth of the thing, the truth of *being* (ὄντος). Whatever is, has ontological truth; for, it contains all that is required to make it what it is.

Again, we may say of our orator, that his thoughts are true, meaning that his notions, judgments, conclusions, correspond to certain things, principles, which are not his thoughts. This second correspondence, namely of thought with thing (meaning by *thing*, whatever can be thought of) is called logical truth, truth of thought, of the λόγος. Finally, we will say that the orator's words are true, meaning, in general, that they correspond with his thoughts—presuming, of course, that the thoughts correspond with things. This correspondence of words with thought is called moral truth. It is called moral truth to indicate the free will that motives the correspondence of the words with the thought: and the opposite of moral truth, that is, falsehood, is said to exist then only when by free will the words are made to disagree with the thought. The thought may, indeed, disagree with thing, there may be logical error; but provided the words are not wilfully made to disagree with the thought, there is still moral truth. The falsehood in such case is purely material, that is, there is simply matter for falsehood. But there is no formal falsehood, because there is absent the form or characteristic of falsehood, that is, the *wilful* deviation from the correspondence which words should naturally have with things through thought.

44. Truth, a Certain Correspondence or Conformity. From this we discover that, in the universal acceptation of terms, truth is understood to be a certain correspondence or conformity. And we would remark, in passing, that in matters philosophical a positive value is to be attached to the constant, universal acceptance of the meaning of words—words being the natural medium for the communication of thought. Hence, though it is easy to err when one too broadly assumes the conditions of the oral word as the measure of the conditions of the mental word; nevertheless, when due discretion is used, we can, from a uniform, constant, universal usage in speech, be sometimes guided to the discovery of an important general principle regarding truth,

45. Logical Truth. This Treatise has to do with logical truth, exclusively. Logical truth is the conformity of thought with *thing*. By *thing* we mean anything whatsoever: any fact, event or abstract principle; any thought, even, that is made the object of another thought. In what, precisely, the conformity consists, we are not called upon to declare further than that the thought answers, as thought can, to the thing thought of. Some new writers have been too ready to reject this term, conformity, as expressive of logical truth, though our definition is founded upon and drawn from the uniform consent of the human race and the practical needs of humanity. The reason why the definition is opposed by these writers is this: to be able, say they, to discover such conformity and thus to be able to know that we have logical truth, it would be necessary to be able to stand off, as it were, so as to survey thought and thing and thus judge whether there existed a likeness between them. But the objection is not reasonable. Thought has its own natural representative-value, as words have their arbitrary representative-value. Whilst reading the interesting page or listening to the vivid discourse, you are carried to the thing represented without adverting to the arbitrary sign, the written or spoken language. And why so? Because of the conformity between the language and the thing written or spoken of. Look at your page and, then, at the blooming valley which it describes. They present no points of similarity to the eye. You will find between them no such conformity as that which exists between portrait and sitter. Yet the printed page conforms to the landscape. Now, if there can be a conformity between language and thing, how much more perfect will be the conformity of thought for which speech is but a poor delegate! And those very writers who object to our definition will still appeal for the truth of their own words to the conformity which they hold those words to have with thought and thing. To admit a conformity, then, it is not necessary to set the thought down beside the thing, and compare the two. In listening to the words of another, without reverting to those words we catch the thought of another; and without reverting to that thought we form our own thought; and without reverting to our own thought we perceive thing, we know thing. We have here a series of conformities, going round like the seamless links of a circular chain from object to the speaker's thought, from his thought to his words, from his words to my thought, from my thought back to object.

Thought is an exercise of mental activity: it is, at the same time, representative; and in it and by it we perceive the object of the thought, without perceiving the thought itself. Now, when the thought is such that in it and by it we really perceive what we believe we do perceive, the thought is said to be true, and we have *logical* truth. It is not necessary for logical truth that the thought embrace the entire object: to what extent there is conformity, to that extent is there logical truth.

46. Logical Falsity. Any positive disagreement between thought and thing is logical falsity. A mere absence of agreement or a total absence of all thought about the object is not falsity or error. Neither is the mere not knowing more about the object—the mere limitation of the scope of our knowledge—error. Our thoughts about a thing may be true and only true, and, yet, fall short of the whole truth. I may not know that the square of the hypothenuse of a right triangle is equal to the sum of the squares of the other sides. This is a mere negative or privative condition of my knowledge, and does not constitute logical falsity. But if I believe that the square of any side in any triangle is equal to the sum of the squares of the other two sides, there is here a positive thought disagreeing with the objective or ontological truth: there is logical falsity, error.

47. Logical Truth: in what Mental Act is it Found? In the "Laws of Thought" we described, briefly, three mental cognitive acts or performances: the simple apprehension, the judgment, and the argumentation or reasoning. The description there given is amply sufficient for the purposes of this work, since we are not occupying ourselves with the essential distinction between the powers of sense-cognition and the power of purely intellectual cognition, though we have to insist, even here (and more fully a little later), upon their being individually distinct. The complete discussion of their essential distinction belongs to psychology.

The simple apprehension was described as the mental act considered in so far only as it contains what corresponds to an oral term, as *man*, *zebra*, *tree*, *blue*, *red, redness, virtue, hope*—without any affirmation or negation connected therewith.

The judgment was described as the mental act whose oral expression is a proposition containing an affirmation or a negation, as, *man is intelligent, hope is a virtue.*

Argumentation or reasoning was described as the mental act which compares objectively the content of two judgments, so as to formulate explicitly a third judgment, whose content was implicitly perceived in the act of comparing,—the oral expression of the act of comparing being the syllogism. Thus:

All virtues are desirable;
Temperance is a virtue;
Therefore, **Temperance is desirable.**

In each of these, apprehension, judgment, reasoning, we have a mental act which is, in its own way, representative, conformable to thing. But which of them is conformable in such a manner that it may be said to contain logical truth—considering the universally accepted meaning of words? We insist upon the universally acccepted meaning of words. Man has always tried to use words in a definite way to express his thought; and we are considering the humanity that is and has been and will be; not an imaginary and impossible humanity. And language, when in universal accord, is, even though of a different order, a very good auxiliary when we have to pass judgment upon thought. In which act, then, is the logical truth? It is not easy for us to tell whether we might so manage the mental act as to hold the apprehension, pure and simple, without formulating a judgment. But whether we might be able to do so or not, no one will venture to say that there is a *complete* truth contained in the apprehension. If you utter merely a term that stands for an apprehension, or even a list of terms, as *temperance*, *desirable*, *virtue*, no person will credit you with a truth or charge you with an error.

But take a proposition, which is the oral expression of the judgment. Take an analytic proposition, such as *parallel lines produced will never meet;* or a synthetic proposition, such as *the sky is dark.* According to the universal usage of words either proposition may be regarded as containing a complete truth: the analytic proposition, at all times; the synthetic, whenever the sky happens to be dark. Anyone will always be ready to declare that a proposition is necessarily either true or false; whilst a simple apprehension or a term will never be called true or false. Now the proposition is nothing more than the oral expression of the mental act of judgment. Hence the mental act of judgment, *parallel lines produced will never meet*, will always be regarded as mentally true, that is, logically true; and the mental act of judgment, *the sky is dark*, the synthetic judgment, will always be regarded as necessarily either true or false logically. Hence we say that logical truth is found complete in the judgment.

48. The Radical Reason. The radical reason why we say that logical truth is found complete in the judgment and not in the apprehension, is because a complete conformity is found in the judgment and not in the apprehension. That which is represented by the simple apprehension or the term is never found out of the mind, isolated and by itself, as it stands in the solitary apprehension and term, but it is found necessarily connected with something else which is also expressible by another apprehension and by another term. For example, that which we call red, objectively, and which is an object of apprehension and can be expressed by the term *red*, does not exist objectively by itself, but naturally conjoined with a something which is red. The objective or ontological truth is not merely *red*, nor merely *something*, but the two conjoined, *something red*. And the apprehension of these two conjoined, as conjoined, is the work of the mental act which is expressed orally by the proposition, *that is red*. This act is the judgment.

We do not say, we repeat it, that there is no element of logical truth in the simple apprehension, since the simple apprehension is, after all, an element of the judgment; but we do not know that we ever make a direct perception and thus form an individual, solitary, isolated notion. The fact is, that, as far as our observation can go, we find ourselves making what I might call a duplex or triplex or quadruplex apprehension. Whatever formality (Laws of Thought, 20) we apprehend directly, we spontaneously attach to it objectively some other formality which constitutes material for another simple apprehension. We apprehend it as actual or possible or past or present or future, as *a* something or *that* something, or even as impossible. There is a dispute among philosophers as to whether over and above the perception of the objective agreement or disagreement of two concepts, the complete judgment requires a new act, which consists in the formal affirmation or denial; or whether the perception itself of agreement or disagreement does not in itself constitute essentially the act of affirmation or denial which we designate judgment. In my opinion, the act of perception is itself essentially what we call the act of affirmation or denial. A new act seems to me to be an unnecessary addition. When we have perceived the agreement or disagreement we have knowledge. The terms affirmation and denial are drawn from the verbal, oral expresion which we give to our mental acts. We speak, indeed, in affirmations and denials; but we think in perceptions. The perception of the objective agreement or disagreement is the mental act of judgment; it is, to use borrowed words, the mental utterance or declaration. The oral expression of agreement or disagreement perceived (an expression effected by means of the affirmative or negative copula) is the verbal judgment or proposition.

Finally, we may remark that as logical truth can exist complete in the judgment, so there can be as many complete logical truths in an argumentation as there are simple judgments contained therein.

Our remarks upon error or logical falsity we reserve for a later chapter.

CHAPTER VIII. CERTITUDE.

Three States of Mind: Ignorance, Doubt, Certitude—Object of Certitude—Three Orders of Ontological Truth: Metaphysical, Physical, Moral—Metaphysical, Physical and Moral Certitude—Objective Certitude—Species and Degrees of Certitude—Certitude: Immediate and Mediate; Direct and Reflex; Philosophical—Probability.

49. Three States of the Mind: Ignorance, Doubt, Certitude. Having determined upon what we mean by logical truth, we may go on to consider the different states of confidence or distrust that may sway the mind with regard to the logical truth contained in a given judgment.

Take two contradictory propositions, "*The number of the stars is odd,*" "*The number of the stars is even.*" One or the other of them must be true; but we have no evidence, positive or negative, for or against either. This leaves us in absolute ignorance with regard to each. Hence when, in contemplating a given proposition, the mind finds no reason whatever to affirm either it or its contradictory, the state of the mind with regard to such proposition, such judgment represented by the proposition, and hence with regard to the possible objective or ontological truth corresponding, is said to be *ignorance*.

When, however, the mind sees positive reasons for affirming each of two contradictories, that is, for affirming and denying the same thing, but dares not adhere to either because it cannot reject the evidence on the other side, it is held in suspense between the two, and is said to be in a state of *doubt*. When, in this state of suspense, the mind does, for grave reasons, incline *more* to one side than to another, yet fearing all the while that the truth may be on the other side, it is said to hold an *opinion*. Thus, two minds looking at the same proposition with different degrees of information may, as we so often see they do, hold different opinions upon the same subject. And the same mind, holding one opinion to-day, may, for new reasons perceived, hold the contradictory opinion to-morrow.

When a proposition is seen to be true, to represent an evident ontological truth, and the contradictory to be evidently false, the mind is established in a state of *certitude* with regard to the evident truth. Certitude is, therefore, a firm assent of the mind to one of two contradictories, without any fear of error.

It may, indeed, happen that two persons may claim to have certitude: the one, of a certain proposition; the other, of the contradictory. This only indicates that one of the persons is judging on insufficient motives; for one of the contradictories must be false. Hence the person holding it must be judging without sufficient consideration.

50. Object of Certitude. It is to be remarked that in rational philosophy we speak of natural certitude only, and not of certitude by divine faith founded on divine testimony. Natural certitude embraces in its adequate object whatever may be known by the natural powers of mind—whether it be concrete fact or general principle. This object, then, is not to be understood as comprising the entire ontological truth, but only that portion which can be naturally known by the human mind. It thus excludes every truth the knowledge of which is absolutely beyond the natural reach of the human mind. Not that any human effort of any mind or of all the human family will ever reach more than a very small fraction of the truths contained in the con-natural adequate object of human certitude; the object embraces, nevertheless, all that lies absolutely within the natural reach of human intelligence.

51. Three Orders of Ontological Truth: Metaphysical, Physical, Moral. We may divide the object of certitude into two classes of ontological truths: one embracing all *general* principles; and the other all *individual* concrete facts or possibilities, past, present or future. The general principles we may again divide into the absolute and the hypothetical. The absolute are those whose universality is absolutely necessary in every case from the very nature of the ideas involved, and which can admit of no exception under any conditions whatsoever. These truths are said to be metaphysically necessary, and are called metaphysical truths. This truth, "*The three angles of a triangle are, together, equal to two right angles*," is a metaphysical truth. It is of the *metaphysical* order. There is no case in which the three angles can be equal to more or less than two right angles.

When the universality of the principle is such that it does not grow out of the very nature of the ideas involved, the truth, though acknowledged to be universal, is said to be contingent, or only hypothetically, that is, conditionally necessary. The universality is such that an exception *is possible*, even though the exception may never occur. These contingent universal truths are of two orders. In the one order we have those general laws that govern the sensible universe and into whose application—or the exception—the human will does not enter. Such are all the laws of physics, of gravitation, light, chemistry, mechanics, etc. They are said to be of the physical order. They are contingent, because there is nothing in the nature of things that makes an exception an impossibility. The earth revolves around the sun. But who will say that it is absolutely necessary that it should do so? It does so by reason of an impulse it has received. But why should not He who gave the impulse have the power to arrest it, or to change the impulse, and make the earth spin and circle in the other direction? We do not say that it will be so. But the law as it exists does not imply the absolute impossibility of the contradictory, and that suffices to keep these truths out of the metaphysical order and to put them in an order of their own, which we call the *physical* order.

The other order of contingent universal truths is that whereinto the human will enters, both for the universality of the truths and the exception therefrom. There are some modes of action, free action, so common to all men in given circumstances, that we can formulate as general laws certain universal truths, regarding some deeds that men will do in those given circumstances. Truths of this kind are, for instance, "Parents will support their children," "My creditor will accept payment when it is due," "A respectable man whom I may accost upon the street will, in answer to my request, give me the correct time of day if he is able." However, these truths admit of the possibility of an exception. They depend for their universality upon the *free human will*. This dependence is indicated by their being termed universal truths of the *moral* order.

The metaphysical universal truths are absolutely necessary; the physical and moral, hypothetically necessary. The necessity in the moral order is weaker than in the physical; and the necessity in the physical, weaker than that in the metaphysical.

What about individual facts? Any individual fact is always equivalent to a general truth of the metaphysical order; for, being a fact, as such it cannot be other than the fact that it is.

52. Metaphysical, Physical, Moral Certitude. Certitude is sometimes denominated metaphysical, physical or moral, according to the order of the ontological truth adhered to. The certitude itself is not metaphysical, physical or moral; but when we so designate it we wish merely to indicate certitude regarding truth of the metaphysical, physical or moral order. These qualifying terms, then, regard strictly only the *truth known*; and they represent something that is altogether extrinsic to certitude which is a state of the mind. Hence certitude, thus spoken of, is said to be qualified by what is technically called an extrinsic denomination.

53. Objective Certitude. Just as we qualify the state of the mind knowing, by terms belonging to the object known; so, also, do we sometimes find the term, certitude, which expresses the state of mind knowing, applied to the object known. The truth or object known is then called *objective* certitude, to distinguish it from the state of mind knowing, which by way of distinction is called *subjective* certitude. We shall find it more convenient to limit the name, *certitude*, to its original signification of the state of mind. We shall thus avoid a possible ambiguity in philosophical terminology. We have, besides, a well understood term to express what is meant by objective certitude, the word *certainty*. With the word *certitude* to express the state of the mind knowing, and *certainty* to express the truth known, much confusion may be avoided. A certainty will thus always signify a truth known, and, certainty, in the abstract, will signify ascertained truth in general. And though we do find the word, certainty, employed in common speech to signify the subjective state of certitude, as in the expressions "to have, to obtain, to arrive at certainty," this need not affect the limitation which we give to the word in philosophical terminology. It may be added that the word "certain," employed as a predicate, has in common language obtained use in the subjective and objective sense as well as in the indefinite (impersonal) sense. We say "I am certain," "that is certain," "it is certain that——."

54. Species and Degrees of Certitude. Some writers have contended that, as there are different orders of truths, truths absolute, *i. e.*, of the metaphysical order, and truths hypothetical, *i. e.*, truths of the physical and moral order—some writers have contended that, therefore, there must be different species of certitude, different species in the assent. The argument brought forward to uphold these different species in the assent is this: that the motives determining the assent vary in the different orders of truth. The motive determining our assent to an ontological truth is the perceived evidence, the perceived objective identification of predicate with subject. This identification, as we have seen, may be absolute or hypothetical. Hence, it is argued, the assent given to the absolute or metaphysical truth must differ from the assent given to the physical or moral truth; and that which is given to the physical must differ from that which is given to the moral, on account of the less liability to exception in the physical than in the moral. But the argument is not fair. It is based upon the transfer of the term, certitude, from the mind to the object. Certitude belongs to the mind and expresses a state of the mind. It is not fair, then, when we find absolute and hypothetical features in the different orders or species of the objective truth, to argue from the borrowed name by which the objective truth is called objective certitude to the conclusion that, therefore, are there different species of mental assent to the connection of subject and predicate as perceived in the ontological truth. It cannot be denied that in the assent we recognize the possibility of exception in the physical and moral general principle as perceived, and the impossibility of exception in the metaphysical principle as perceived. But this does not make any difference. For the argument overlooks the important fact that, when we assent to a truth, we assent to its entirety as presented to us and as evident to us. Now, the entirety of the truth presented to us and as evident to us in the one case (metaphysical) is, a-general-truth-which-admits-absolutely-of-no-exception; and in the other case (physical and moral) it is a-general-truth-which-may-absolutely-admit-of-an-exception. Hence, when I have certitude in regard to truths of both kinds, I hold to the one truth as being in its entirety an absolute truth, in the very same way that I hold to the other truth as being in its entirety a hypothetical truth. Hence, though there may be different grades of necessity in the connection between subject and predicate objectively in truths of the different orders, yet this necessity affects only the truth perceived and not the mind perceiving.

There are other writers, again, who, recognizing that there is but one kind or species of certitude, still wish to introduce various degrees of *intensity*, in the firm assent. First, they distinguish the two quasi-elements of certitude; the positive element, which is the holding to the truth known; and the negative element, which is the absence of all apprehension in regard to the correctness of the judgment formed. Mere absence, in so far as it is mere absence, they see very well, does not admit of degrees, since it is a negation. But they wish to have degrees of intensity in the positive holding, so that though a person may be absolutely certain of a truth, that person's certainty in regard to the same truth may grow more intense; and so, that a person having absolute certainty of a metaphysical and of a physical truth may yet attain a more intense certainty regarding the one than regarding the other, and vice versa. However, there is here introduced a complication which we do not feel inclined to recognize, notwithstanding the dignity of the writers who have repeated it. What the writers in question really mean is simply this: that new light is thrown upon the truth. They affirm (and they stop short at the affirmation) that if one person has, for instance, three independent arguments or evidences, each of which is sufficient to establish certitude, and another person has only one of the three, or if the same person advances by study from one sufficient motive to three, the assent will be more intense with the three motives than with the one alone, although that one gave complete certitude and quiet of mind. It is not easy to see how the two extra motives will affect the intensity of the assent. If I am really certain, I am certain, and there is an end to the matter. I may get a hundred new motives, but they will not affect the intensity of my assent. They may, perhaps, set me at rest regarding possible difficulties that might be made against the truth and for which I might not have a ready answer. They will give me a wider knowledge of the various connections of the truth in question; and this is a result that always accompanies study. But where once there is assent, there is assent; where there is certitude, there is certitude, and it cannot be intensified. When once you have proved that the square erected on the hypothenuse of a right triangle is equal to the sum of the squares erected on the two other sides, your certainty of the truth is as intense as it will be when you have learned ten other proofs. The ten new proofs may afford you scientific satisfaction, but they will not affect your certitude.

Attention is called to a very broad use of the word "moral" in connection with certitude. We often find the expression "moral certitude" ("moral certainty") employed to indicate a very strong opinion for which the arguments are so weighty that the arguments against it may be regarded as only specious, though the absolute refutation of them cannot be readily accomplished.

55. Certitude: Immediate and Mediate; Direct and Reflex; Philosophical. Certitude is called immediate when we assent to a truth which is perceived as presented to us *in itself* and not *through a medium*. It is called mediate when the assent is given to a truth which has been perceived through a medinm, through a demonstration, for instance, or the testimony of a recognized authority.

Certitude, whether immediate or mediate, when first arising, is called *direct* certitude, to distinguish it from what is termed *reflex* certitude, which is the state of the mind following the satisfactory investigation or "proof" of the motives upon which the direct certitude was based.

This investigation may, of course, be made in a more or less elaborate manner; and it is as a rule made in a degree by all men, upon the apprehension of truths that are new to them. We say in common language that we look or think or listen *twice* to be certain. When this investigation is carried into details so as to consider the nature of the truth presented, the kind of necessity existing in the connection between the predicate and the subject, the precise perceptive conditions of the faculty through which the truth is first ushered into the domain of knowledge, and also of the other faculties by which it is elevated into the spiritual regions of thought, and finally the point where investigation must cease if we will not quench all light of knowledge in the mists of absolute scepticism—then we arrive at what is dignified by the name of *philosophical* certitude.

56. Probability. We have spoken of doubt as a hesitation of the mind between two contradictories; and of opinion, as a leaning of the mind to one of the contradictories for reasons which seem more cogent, but which do not, nevertheless, refute the arguments for the other contradictory. Probability is the capacity for proof or demonstration, the plea for acceptance in a doubtful case. The probability of a proposition is the weight or value of the sum of argument that can be brought forward in an endeavor to establish the proposition. Of course, if the proposition can be logically established, and its contradictory can be logically shown to be false, we then have a true proposition representing a certified ontological or objective truth. But if we cannot establish the falsity of the contradictory, then the proposition remains only probable; and its probability will vary with the weight of argument that can be advanced for it. Thus we can hold only an opinion as to its representing an ontological truth. Hence, according to the weight of argument, we will say that a proposition is hardly probable, simply probable, very probable, extremely probable.

Probability, strictly taken, refers to that which is to be proved. But, by a transfer of terms, we apply the word, probable, to the opinion itself—that is, to the state of mind inclining, for reasons, to a probable proposition. We speak of a probable opinion, a very probable opinion, etc.

Moreover, as the proposition stands for the judgment, and the judgment and proposition stand for the ontological order, we also employ the terms, probable and probability, when speaking of that which the probable proposition is intended to represent. We speak of a probable cause, a probable effect, a probability—meaning that there are for said cause, effect, etc., arguments weighty enough to justify one in forming an opinion.

CHAPTER IX. MEANS WE POSSESS FOR ACQUIRING KNOWLEDGE—PERCEPTIVE OR KNOWING POWERS—THE EXTERNAL SENSES.

A Difficulty—Unity of the Human Person—The Outer Senses—The Formal Objects of the Outer Senses—Taste—Smell —Hearing—Sight—Touch.

57. A Difficulty. It is necessary for us to say something, in this treatise, about the means with which nature has provided us for arriving at knowledge. But in determining upon what to say, we are forced to put the balance of our discrimination to the most exquisite test. It is of the very last importance that we do not introduce into our treatise what does not belong to it. Yet, as we face the present subject, we find ourselves upon the borders of sciences that require, each, a distinct and separate treatment. When we touch upon the knowledge of the abstract, the perception of universal truths, and the power of comparing judgments for the sake of drawing conclusions, we are apt to run into rational psychology and to institute inquiries into the nature of the principle that can know the immaterial, as distinct from, or discriminated, in some way, from the principle that can know only the individual, the concrete, the material. And, when we touch upon sense-perception, we run the risk of extending our remarks into mutilated treatises upon anatomy, physiology, optics, accoustics, etc. In beginning this book we made up our mind that it should not be written from what we may call the point of view of the specialist—from any outside technical standpoint. We stand upon the common ground of humanity. However, in steering clear of the Scylla of exuberance we are in danger of striking the Charybdis of barrenness. We must, therefore, try, at least, to be careful; and it may be useful for us to bear in mind what is contained in the following paragraph.

58. Unity of the Human Person. Let it be understood, once for all, that in this treatise we are not called upon to prove the nature of the soul or the nature of the body. But we are called upon to hold what consciousness presents to us, namely, the *unity of the totality of man*. The unit, *Ego*, *I*, is the subject of each individual predication and of the sum total of all the predications made by consciousness. If there is thinking, it is *I* that think, not the mind; but I think by the use of the power or faculty of thinking which belongs to *me*, and which we call mind, intellect, reason. When there is judgment, I judge. When there is hearing, I hear. The hearing belongs to me, not to the ear. The ear is nothing in the perceptive order except in so far as it belongs to the vital me. So, also, it is not the eye that sees, but I see. And so it is with every predication of every exercise of a capacity for action belonging to the human person. I think, I will, I see, I walk, I hope, I sleep, I fall, etc.

59. The Outer Senses. We have previously said enough about consciousness, the power we possess of knowing self and the modifications of self. The study of self, by this power of consciousness, shows us that we are put into communication, perceptive communication, with the outer world of matter by means of five distinct organs or sets of organs which form parts of the body belonging to self. These organs are eyes, ears, nostrils, tongue-and-palate, entire-body-surface. These organs, when vivified by that ever identical unit, the principle of life that is within us, are constituted senses; and in them and through them the vital principle becomes first perceptive of the outer world of matter. The five senses or perceptive powers, thus constituted, are called, respectively, sight, hearing, smell, taste, touch. This is a very old division of the outer senses; as old, indeed, as man. We find the exercise of the five senses recorded in the first chapters of Genesis; and we find no new outer sense discovered up to the present time. It is true the sense of touch has been subdivided as to the qualities perceived, temperature, movement, resistance. The power of perceiving resistance and movement is styled muscular sense, and the sense of *touch proper* is limited to the perception of mere contact. Howsoever the case may be, the distinction is sufficiently vague even to physiologists, and we are justified, for our present purposes, in including all the subdivisions under the single name of touch. The power of exercising sense-perception is called, in general, *sensibility* or simply *sense*.

60. The Formal Objects of the Outer Senses. We may very well marvel when we come to consider how the vast stores of knowledge accumulated in the minds and the libraries of men have been built up, manufactured, as it were, to use a material expression, out of what is provided by the exercise of sense-perception. And the wonder only grows when we find upon investigation how very, very limited is the object upon which each sense is privileged to exercise itself. The formal object of any sense, as of any perceptive power, is that form, formality, determination, peculiarity, something, which the sense perceives immediately and directly, without which it could not exercise its perceptive power, and which, as residing in concrete matter here and there (material object), is the reason why the sense is said to perceive the object in which that form or formality resides. It is out of the perception of the formal objects of the faculties that we construct, so to say, the stores of knowledge which we lay by. We shall here consider briefly the formal objects of the several external senses.

61. Taste. Though we know sufficiently well, for the practical purposes of life, what we mean when we say that an object has a *taste*, yet, when we come to speak philosophically, we find it hard to define accurately what we mean by the formal object of the sense of taste. We certainly do not taste light or sound or extension. As far as we know, the formal object of taste is a certain variable quality which some bodies possess, when in solution, of affecting the tongue and palate in such a way (chemically, perhaps) as to put the tongue and palate in that condition in which they are when we say we *taste*. This formal object we should be inclined to call *sapor*, in order to give it a distinctive name. It is commonly called taste, for we say that things have a bitter taste or a sour taste; but thus we are using the same word for the sense and the object. We might call it flavor or savor; but these too readily suggest the element of agreeableness from which we must abstract when we wish to express in one word that character in matter which can furnish, whether as agreeable, disagreeable or indifferent, what is essential for the exercise of the sense of taste.

Taste and smell are closely allied; and, in swallowing, sensations of smell may be mistaken for sensations of taste. The word, taste, is sometimes incorrectly used for touch, as when, for instance, acid is said to have a burning taste. In the same way we speak of a nauseous taste or a nauseous smell, whereas nausea is a revolt of the alimentary canal.

The knowledge derived through taste is very slight. It is, indeed, held very generally that the sensation of taste is purely subjective—that is, that by the act of taste we do not perceive objective reality, do not get at the not-self, but perceive merely the modification of self. And it is said that were it not for the exercise of touch or sight upon the object tasted, from which, after repeated experiences, we infer the existence of something objective whenever there is a sensation of taste, we should get from taste no knowledge whatever of objective reality. However the case may be, we are not willing to spend our time, here, upon mere theory, be it ever so plausible. If by the aid of sight and touch we can, through inference, assert the objectivity of the formal object of taste, we are ready to let the matter go at that. Nevertheless, we may very well ask whether there be not here, as in the exercise of every external faculty whose exercise is intimately connected with the preservation of human life, some perception of the *not-self* character of the object. Take the case of an infant of six months. It will try to rid itself of a disagreeable taste remaining in its mouth, though it has no perception whatever beyond mere taste, and there is nothing in its mouth upon which *touch* might seem to be exercised. Shall we say that the infant is drawing an inference from the experience it has had of taste being exercised upon that which touch has revealed as not-self, and is thus somehow deciding that there is now in its mouth an object which is of the character of not-self and which may be removed to a convenient distance? Or has it direct perception of not-self through taste alone? I should very much like to know. Could we obtain a history of the first developments of child knowledge, we should find therein the simple solution of some problems of psychology which have baffled the genius of all philosophers, and which still remain an open challenge to the philosophers of the rest of time.

One thing we may note. Remarkably meager as is the direct knowledge we get from taste, no less remarkable is the wide adaptation we make of the variations in the formal object of taste in order to enrich our vocabulary, when wishing to characterize objects (howsoever perceived) that influence the emotions. Thus we have now almost lost sight of the metaphorical origin of epithets in such expressions as, a sour look, a bitter retort, a sweet child, an insipid story, etc.

62. Smell. The organ of the sense of smell is the membranous lining of the nostrils.

The formal object of smell is that variable quality in bodies, which we designate by the common term, odor. In order that the sense of smell may be exercised upon a body, particles of the body possessing the quality we call odor must come in contact with the organ. The minuteness of the quantity of a body required for the sense of smell to exercise itself upon is seen in the well-known case of the grain of musk, which will for years emit particles perceptible to smell, and yet will not show any diminution of weight when tested by the most delicate balance. The sense of smell is very closely allied to taste. It acts as a valuable companion, a guide. It goes before taste with its keen discernment to warn and to encourage. It thus plays a directive part in the conservation of animal life by giving a preliminary hint for the choice and rejection of food. It also subserves the office of taste by saving the latter from many disagreeable experiences. As the particles containing the odor perceived are carried to the organ of smell by the atmosphere, smell will, evidently, enable us to reach further than will taste, in detecting, at least by inference, the existence—though distant—of an odorous body from which the particles come.

Of course, the same difficulty confronts us here that we met with in the case of taste. Does smell directly perceive external reality, or have we, in it, simply the consciousness of a peculiar modification of self? The general sentiment is that there is no direct perception of external reality, but that our judgment of the existence of an odorous body which we can neither touch nor see, is an inference drawn from a general law which we have established after varied experience. If this be so, we are thrown headlong into that unfathomable question: How soon does the infant draw inference from personal experience? We are left in the abyss without light for exploration. Yet if, under the supposition, we will deny to the infant this power of drawing an inference from its own experiences, even before it is a year old, we shall have no little difficulty in explaining many of its actions. We may even have to fall back upon the direct perception of external reality by the sense of smell. Why does the infant turn its head away from a substance that has a disagreeable odor? Why, even with its eyes closed, will it turn its head away? May it not, perhaps, by the sense of smell perceive directly some externality?

On account of the close alliance between smell and taste we find the same epithets applied to the objects of each. So closely, indeed, are the two allied in the economy of life that it is sometimes not easy to say whether the sensation experienced is one of taste or of smell.

63. Hearing. The formal object of the sense of hearing is that something which we call sound. Outside of us, in so far as we know, sound is a vibration of matter. These vibrations of what we call the sounding body are communicated to the surrounding atmosphere, thence to the tympanum of the ear, from this to the series of small bones in the middle ear, from these to the liquid in the labyrinth of the inner ear, and thence to the auditory nerve; then we hear. Our notion of vibration and our notion of sound are two quite different things. We do not hear those vibrations which we find so essentially connected with the sound. It is only in the study of physics that we have learned of the existence of such vibrations. Whether there be outside of us something accompanying the vibration, caused by the vibration and distinct from it, and which is the object, *sound*, which we hear, or whether sound is purely the manner in which the vibration of external matter affects the sense of hearing, we do not know.

We perceive differences of sound. Some of these are differences of *pitch*, which depends upon the rapidity of the vibrations in the sounding body. The pitch is said to be lower as the vibrations are fewer in a given time, and higher as the number increases in the same time. We designate as noise, a sound whose pitch cannot be determined. There are, again, differences of *timbre*, which depends upon the material or construction of the vibrating body. By hearing we can also perceive that variety in the succession of sounds which we call melody, and that combination of sounds which we call harmony.

The organ of hearing acts with great rapidity. We can recognize as many as sixteen distinct successive sounds in a second.

The great value of the sense of hearing in the economy of life lies in its perception and discrimination of the articulate sounds emitted by the human voice. It is by the perception of these, more than by anything else, that we are put into communication with our fellow men. A certain few articulate sounds which, taken singly and in groups of various combinations, are called words and are accepted as signs for things, give us the marvellous vehicle of speech upon which society rides.

Do we perceive distance and direction by hearing? It may be said safely that we have no direct perception of distance by hearing. When we cannot see or touch the object producing the sound, our estimate of its distance must be purely a matter of judgment based upon our experience of the variation in the intensity corresponding to the known variation in the distance of the object from which the sound proceeds. Yet, even in this case, we should be able to judge of that sound only whose intensity is invariable at a given known distance and which is known to be unmodified by accidental circumstances such as the humid state of the atmosphere, the presence or absence of reflecting surfaces, etc. On the other hand, it may be positively stated that we have some direct perception of direction by hearing. This, however, would seem to arise from the independent action of the two ears. We judge very accurately whether a mosquito is playing his overture at our right ear or at our left. This species of perception seems to be in the kind economy of nature, and manifests itself very early with the development of the organs of hearing.

64. Sight. The organ of sight is the eye. The formal object of sight is light. We see light according to the various modes in which it is partially or entirely reflected to the eye after falling on material substance. When the light (sunlight) is perfectly reflected to the eye, we perceive what we call *white*. When the light is divided on striking the substance and only part of it is reflected, we perceive what we call *color*. When there is absolutely no reflection of light rays, the perception is of *black;* or, to speak strictly, there is no perception. As a pure white is so rare upon the objects we see around us, the formal object of vision is frequently said to be colored surface. Take the whitest piece of paper you can find and hold it up between you and the new-fallen snow, and see how dark the paper is. The varied perception of what we style color is due to the varying effect of the divided light rays on the optic nerve. Of course, we are speaking broadly, as we cannot enter into the details of the organ of vision. When substances having different powers of absorbing and reflecting the component elements of white light are mixed, they assume a compound power (so to say) of absorption and reflection and give us the opportunity to perceive new *shades* of color. This composition of reflected rays may be said to correspond in a way to the composition of sound vibrations that occasions for the ear the sensation of harmony.

As light is spread over surface we perceive the light as extended. Hence by sight we perceive the outlines of figures. But here there is something to be remarked which is not generally known: By sight we perceive extension *merely as if it were the extension of a plane, flat surface, perpendicular to the axis of vision.* This may seem very strange; but it is true. Sight gives us no knowledge of distance except as on a plane perpendicular to the axis of vision. The whole world lighted up outside of us is perceived by the eye as perfectly flat—flat as the wall before you. The beautiful landscape you look upon—the broad meadows, the parks and villas, the sweep of waters beyond and the background of deep forest and receding mountains—are for you, in so far as the eye is concerned, simply as so many flat outlined sections with shades of color, all as though on one flat surface of canvas hung up before you. The knowledge of distance—except of distance on the flat surface perpendicular to the axis of vision—the knowledge of the practical effects of perspective, of the relative size and of the nearness or remoteness of objects which reflect light (or do not reflect it) is supplied *altogether independently of vision.* It is supplied originally by touch and locomotion. When the infant first opens its eyes and distinguishes between the brightness of colors reflected to its eye, all is as on a flat surface. In thinking of what is herein implied we may well marvel at the education of nature. The infant is carried about in the arms of its nurse. It is taught to reach out its hand for an object presented to it. It is carried to the window and sees the objects in the room disappear behind it. It is brought out into the street for a long promenade. Objects that seemed to be on a flat surface are found not to be so. They are reached one after another. Objects that seemed to be small are found to be large when, after some locomotion, they are reached and the hand can be placed upon them. What at first seemed to be only a dark shade on a flat surface is found by touch and locomotion to mark a recess, and what seemed to be only a brighter spot upon the surface is recognized to mark a prominence. The converging lines of perspective in the rows of houses are found not to be a reality. It is discovered, after locomotion, that the lines do not converge. And thus, gradually, under the tuition of nature, the child is led to draw inferences regarding distance. From its knowledge acquired through touch and locomotion and with its very primary perception of time—a before and an after held by memory—whilst moving from place to place, it comes unconsciously to combine shades and converging lines in such a way as to judge of relative distances and depths and sizes. Look at a well-made photograph of the rows of columns in an arcade or a gothic cathedral. You have the perspective perfect, though you are looking at a flat surface. Or take the case of a stage-setting. When we have not an experience to guide us we may often find it difficult to say where the reality ends and where the painting on the canvas begins. All this knowledge, then, of distance and perspective is a pure inference drawn with that rapidity to which nature trains us in everything that concerns the needs of human life.

65. Touch. Under the general name of touch we here include not merely that by which we perceive the contact of external matter, but also that by which we perceive temperature, as well as what is styled the muscular sense by which we are said to perceive resistance, movement, degrees of elasticity, etc. We do not here consider these as distinct senses. The distinction of senses should be based upon separate organs as clearly discriminated as the eye and the ear, and upon formal objects as readily determinable as light and sound. Physiologists are working towards a distinction, but as yet they are able to give us only a theory; so that we are fully privileged to include the sense of contact, the sense of temperature and the muscular sense under the common name of touch. Besides, for our present purpose, which is only to indicate some of the externalities which we perceive by means of our bodily organs, it will not matter whether we reduce the sense of touch even to the single name of the sense of contact, and divide and subdivide the object perceived according to modes of contact as we divide and subdivide colors; or whether we make twenty different senses out of what we here designate by the one name, touch. We are not making physiological investigations.

First of all, it is well understood that we can have by the sense of mere contact a tactual perception of the existence of matter external to the body belonging to our own personality—that is, of matter distinct from the matter of our own bodies. The organ of this sense of contact is understood to be the system of papillæ distributed over the entire surface of the human body between the dermis, or under-skin, and the epidermis, the scarf-skin or outer-skin, which covers and protects the whole system of papillæ. These papillæ are connected by the nerve apparatus through the spinal column with the brain. By the same sense of contact, by a double contact, as when placing one hand upon the other, we have also a tactual perception of body-belonging-to-self. Through this double contact, aided by sight, we come to a knowledge of the external conformation of the human body. By this sense of contact we perceive distance in three dimensions. The localization of the part of the body at which there is contact with external matter is learned chiefly by experience, and the degree of precision to which this power of localization can be carried, or, at least, is carried, differs in different parts. Thus, it reaches a high degree of accuracy at the tip of the tongue, while the discernment of the exact spot at which there is contact upon the back is not so easy. We can distinguish simultaneously different points of contact, as on the hand and on the foot. The palm of the hand, by reason of exercise, and, perhaps, by some natural adaptation not easy to explain, is the best tactual instrument we have for the perception of figure outlines. We perceive extension by moving an extended object over a point on the surface of the body, or by passing a point of the surface over the extended object.

It is not very clear what may be the peculiar apparatus we possess for the perception of temperature. The power of perceiving temperature is spread over the whole human body. Moreover, the sensation of temperature may exist when the tactual sense or power of perceiving contact has lost its vigor, and *vice versa*. Our perception of temperature is very relative. An atmosphere that will feel cool to one human body may feel warm to another. If we have habituated ourselves to an atmosphere of 50° and pass to one of 60°, our experience, other things being equal, will be about the same as when we pass from 60° to 70°. Of two persons entering an atmosphere of 60°, the one from 50° and the other from 70°, the first will feel warmth; and the other, cold. Intense heat and cold when fully communicated to the surface are not appreciated as heat and cold, but only as a source of pain. The perception of strain, as in lifting, of resistance and of movement is ascribed to what is called the muscular sense, because the muscles play so great a part in these perceptions. The physiology of the matter is not, however, very clear. Hence, for our present purposes, it has sufficed for us to include this perceptive power under the general name of touch. It is through the movements of the body and its members, combined with contact, that we get at our most precise notions of time, space and velocity. Sight, also, plays a great part in furnishing material for these notions, and, of course, comes to be relied upon, as it reaches farther than touch or the muscular perception. In the life of the child, the education of the sense of touch, taken in its broad meaning, is the most wonderful of all the processes of nature's training of the senses. The exquisite capacity for cultivation residing in touch is manifested in the education of the blind who have to rely so much upon it.

Touch supplemented by sight puts before us the panorama of nature in all its beauty of outline, perspective and coloring.

We may add here that we have a sense-perception of certain facts lying wholly within our bodily organism, and which we do not refer to outside matter. However, we do not perceive all that takes place within the organism. We do not perceive the *regular* circulation of the blood; but an *abnormal* circulation may produce a perceptible effect which we will denominate a headache. Thus we also take congnizance of certain symptoms of disease; of hurts; of hunger, thirst, etc.

CHAPTER X. IMAGINATION.

Imagination—Imagination and Intellect—External Senses and Imagination—Error in the Judgment—The Normal State—Uses of the Imagination.

66. Imagination. To complete the list of organic faculties engaged in the work of knowledge, we shall speak briefly and separately of the imagination. The imagination, as the name indicates, is the power of *imaging* anything of which the *reality* is perceptible to some sense, that is, perceptible to a faculty working necessarily with a material organ. We commonly associate the name, image, with the *visible* representation of a *visible* object. But if we are to keep the name, imagination, for the faculty of which we are now speaking (and the use of the name is universal), it would be just as well to employ the word *image* to signify the object which is perceived by the imagination after being produced by the imagination. This object which terminates the action of the imagination is sometimes called the *phantasm*, that is, phantom-object or appearance. Here again we are using terms that are commonly appropriated to the sense of vision; and this shows us how widely vision enters into the economy of life. Any fictitious perception of that which is the object of *any* sense is the work of the imagination. You can imagine to yourself a sound, a color, figure, odor, taste, though there be at hand no object upon which ear, eye, smell, etc., are being exercised. That image or phantasm or fancy is at once the product of the imagination and the object upon which the imagination exercises itself when making the image stand proxy for a reality.

67. Imagination and Intellect. Confusion of Terms. One of the greatest sources—if not the greatest source—of confusion in philosophy as we find it, is the failure which not a few writers have made to draw a broad dividing line between imagination and intellect. Consequent upon this, of course, is the failure to mark off very distinctly the separate terminology belonging to the two totally distinct faculties. Since the days of Locke the term, *idea*, has been widely employed to express the representation produced by the imagination. But we have said that the imagination is limited to the imaging of that which can be the object of sense-perception. The term, *idea*, on the contrary, has been long consecrated from the days of Aristotle, to signify the *intellectual* representation, something quite different from the phantasm or image, and embracing in its scope not only that which can be the object of sense-perception, but that also which does not fall under the perception of any sense; embracing in its scope *whatsoever* can be known; and, even when it is concerned with things that *do* fall under sense, differing in its make-up from the sense-representation of the same object.

Look at the house across the street. Now, close your eyes and see it *without* looking at it. This is the work of the imagination. Call up in fancy the fragrance of the heliotrope, the strain of music, the soft touch of velvet, the tired feeling after yesterday's promenade. This fiction of the sensible object and of the sense-perception is the work of the imagination. Place before you in image (with your eyes closed) a triangle. This is the fancied *image* of a triangle, not the *idea* of a triangle. The image is always limited to something that is perceptible by some sense; and it is also limited, each time that it acts, to an individual object, or to certain individuals of the kind, just as a photograph will not be a likeness of every person in the city. But the idea, which belongs to the intellect, need not be limited to this or that particular case. Your *idea* of triangle may become so broad as to embrace all triangles and be applicable to any particular possible triangle. Such universality cannot belong to the image or phantom object which is each time as limited as would be the real material object for which it is made to do service. Besides this, we can have ideas or intellectual representations of many things that cannot be reached by sense-perception and imagination, of things that are incapable of being materially represented. Thus, *cause*, *justice*, *hope*, etc., cannot fall under sense-perception, and yet we can have *ideas* of them. Moreover, the idea of a thing that can be perceived by sense and reproduced by the imagination or fancy in image, is something distinct from the image of the same thing. In the idea—even the most primitive idea—we catch, at once, relations as of fitness, proportion, beauty, things which as such cannot make a material impression; and as these relations grow the idea develops and grows, whilst the sense-perception and the image in the fancy remain ever the same. The idea is also called *notion* and *concept*. The idea is the primary element in intellectual knowledge. Pure sense-perception and imagination do not rise above mere brute animal life. They give the bare picture as presented here and now in matter. But the intellect to which the idea belongs does not work with a material organ such as the brain, the eye and the ear. Even when it forms its *idea* of a particular triangle, that is put before the eye or is pictured in the imagination, it goes through a spontaneous and instantaneous process of analysis and synthesis, picking out the essentials of three lines and the enclosed space with three angles. In sense-perception, whether directly by the external senses or by the supplementary work of the imagination, we receive and perceive only individual, present manifestations of matter; in the idea we have, at once, the attempted reply to the question, "what is it?"

The complete discussion of the distinction between the intellect and the imagination and between the idea and the image or phantasm belongs to psychology. But the distinction is of such prime importance and the knowledge of it is so essentially necessary to a correct appreciation of the meaning of conclusions in any department of philosophy, that attention should be called to it very early in the course of philosophical studies.

68. External Sense and Imagination. Illusions. There is no difficulty in distinguishing between perception by the imagination and perception by external sense, between the reality of the object as perceived by the external sense and the phantom character of the object set up and then perceived by the imagination. The object as figured by the imagination is less vivid, less definite and detailed than the object as perceived by the outer sense. Besides, the work of the imagination is subject to the control of the will; you can, even at midnight, imagine a sunset. But you cannot *see* a sunset unless it be really before you, and if it be there and you open your eyes to it you cannot help seeing it.

As for illusions and hallucinations, we make no account of them in this treatise. From these as well as from hasty judgments passed without sufficient evidence a great show of argument is sometimes made to invalidate the testimony of the senses. The following objection we believe to be the strongest that is made; and the solution of it supplies the principles necessary for the solution of all difficulties that are brought forward with the intent of fostering sceptical tendencies.

The whole objection is put briefly thus: A person whose leg has been amputated at the knee may and does sometimes feel pain or experience the contact of external matter at the foot. Now the foot is gone! Hence, if the senses fail in this case, they may fail in any other case and no reliance is to be placed upon them. What is to be said to this? We must simply take all the facts. In the person spoken of there are certain nerves which before the amputation had their terminals in the foot. Through the foot—

and through the foot only—did these nerves reach out to be exercised in the perception of external matter by contact. But we must not forget that it was chiefly through vision and double contact that the person learned very early to refer the point of contact to the proper part of the body—to the foot, by seeing the contact made with external matter or with the hand or with the other foot. Thus it was that a given nerve-excitation which always answered to contact at a given point came to be associated with and referred for its origin to a particular locality where these nerves had their terminals. Now, it comes to pass that these nerves are severed at the knee. The whole stretch of nerve from the knee to the foot disappears. The nerves have new terminals at the knee. What may be the result? The result may be that when there is contact with external matter at the new terminals, as the signal that there is contact will be carried to the nerve-centres along the very same lines as from the old terminals, thus affecting the nerve centre in the same way and occasioning the same reaction as before the amputation, the person, if not very watchful, may, at the beginning, refer the point of contact to the locality of the old terminals, forgetful for the moment of the new. It is done through the force of habit, and it will be necessary to acquire a new habit of referring the stimulus to the new locality of the terminals. In fact, to explain the whole case in a sentence, if the process of amputation and healing could have been gone through, and the person have been kept absolutely ignorant of what had taken place, an external contact which should stimulate only a new terminus of a nerve which had its former terminus for example in the heel, would necessarily be referred to the heel until the person had come to know that the heel was gone. Precisely the same thing will have to be said with regard to the referring of sensations of warmth, cold, pressure, pain, etc., to localities which do not exist, but which did formerly contain the termini of the nerves at present stimulated.

69. Error in the Judgment. It will be readily seen that the error just spoken of is an error of judgment. The expression that our senses deceive us, that our eyes deceive us, is philosophically false. The senses, the eyes, cannot deceive us. The senses testify to just so much as is presented to them, to just so much as they receive. But very often we presume upon our experience and judge things to be what they are not, concluding hastily and rashly from that which we perceive to that which we do not perceive.

70. The Normal State. Of course, then, it will be understood that we have been speaking of the senses in the normal condition of the body. The discussion of the peculiarities of nerve-action in abnormal conditions of the body or of any particular organ, belongs to medicine, to therapeutics, to physiology, to the art of diagnosing disease from its symptoms. Here we have merely to declare and to hold fast that in the normal condition of the system the testimony of any sense and of the imagination is, just as well as that of the intellect, thoroughly reliable for the truthful and infallible recognition of its respective formal object.

71. Uses of the Imagination. Each individual sensation would be as nothing for the growth of knowledge if it simply came and went and left nothing behind. But each individual sensation is re-enforced by the work of memory and imagination which grow in activity and readiness by exercise and throw around each new sensation a host of recollections and associations. In all art the imagination is invaluable, indispensable. It enables the composer to put his work before him in image and to judge of its figure, color, proportion, etc., to reject, to substitute, to modify, to add, etc., without touching or even providing the material. Thus he can, by setting up the phantom-object of the imagination, make, in a moment, the constructive experiment which, if made in the reality, would cost him months, nay years of very unsatisfactory toil.

CHAPTER XI. INTELLECT AND THOUGHT.

The Intellectual Act—The Principle of Unity—Acts of Intellect or Mind—Mediate and Immediate Knowledge—The Idea as a Sign—The Universal Idea: Nominalism, Conceptualism, Realism—Thought.

72. The Intellectual Act. All that has been hitherto said merges as subsidiary into the matter of the present chapter. The perceptive action of the human being, man, differs from the perceptive action of the purely animal being in this, that the purely animal being has only sense-perception, that is, perception whose working is tied down to the use of a material organ, whilst man has, over and above this, a perceptive action which he exercises free from the trammels of eye, ear, nerves, brain, etc. This supra-sensitive knowing capacity, capability or power, is called *intellect*. The very name intellect (from *intus legere*, to read within) declares the character of this higher power. A sense, that is, a power whose working is strictly limited to the working of a material organ, reaches only to its formal object which is some particular outward quality of matter, and each time that the sense does act it has perception merely of the individual quality here and now present to it; its action is as limited, though vital, as the action of a mirror reflecting the various objects that pass before it. The sense, though its actions (like the reflections of the mirror) are successive, takes no cognizance of time as such; and though it may perceive that which is extended, it takes no cognizance of space as such. Though it represents all the points in the figure of the triangle it does not cognize the *nature* of the triangle; it cannot cognize even its own formal object in the abstract and in general, but only as here and now limited to the actual individual case presented to it. It cannot cognize, at all, such things as justice, hope, temperance, causality, possibility, patience, etc., things which are not to be reached by mediate or immediate contact with any nerve terminus. Since, however, we have knowledge of these things, which yet are incapable of acting upon or of being perceived through a material organ, there must be in us a faculty which acts without an organ and which even excludes the intrinsic concurrence of matter in the performance of its peculiar supra-sensitive cognitive act. We say that there is no intrinsic concurrence of matter in the execution of this act. We do not deny the extrinsic concurrence of matter, that is, the prior or simultaneous act of some sense necessarily working with a material organ as sense always does. For there is a sensitive act associated at least remotely with every intellectual act, just as there is an intellectual perception following every sensitive act of knowledge. The imagination, too, a sensitive faculty, keeps up a simultaneous working whilst the thought goes on. It draws its pictures as an aid to the easy sequence of the thought, even restlessly trying to image things that cannot be pictured. But all this object building of the imagination is the work of sense, since it involves necessarily in the very act the concurrence of the cerebral organism. The extrinsic concurrence of sense is a prior necessity to all thought. We can have no intellectual idea of color, for instance, unless we shall have first perceived color by the sense-perception of sight. We hold that all knowledge begins through sense, and we deny even so much as one innate idea. Yet sense-perception is not thought. The act of sense is an act totally different from the act of intellect which accompanies and follows it; and in the intellectual act, the concept, the judgment, the reasoning process, there is no concurrence of matter as there is in the act of sense.

73. The Principle of Unity. We must here hint at a great vital truth of psychology, namely, the bond of unity that exists between the acts of the individual person, in that they all proceed from and are all predicated of, attributed to the one identical subject, the *ego*, the me, self. There must, for this reason, be some principle of unification. There must be a certain one something pervading the whole of each individual human being, a something which besides being one and identical in every atom of that human being (since the temperature of head and of foot, the walk, the thought, etc., all belong to the same identical me) is also the primary agent or principle in each and all of the acts attributed to self (for I think, I walk, I am warm). This primary principle we call the spiritual soul. In its permanency and continuity it primarily constitutes the permanent, continuous self. This soul cannot be matter, for it does what no mere material agent can do. However, it can act with matter as with an instrument. It vivifies the body; and with the body, with the material sense-organs whose life it supplies from its higher domain, it reaches out to the external, material world. But its other acts, the intellectual idea, the judgment, the argument, do not admit matter into their working. Still, it is the one same individual *ego*, self, that claims all the acts. This one self has a permanent root or principle by which it continues to be itself, ever the same. This permanent root or principle is the soul. Some speak of soul as *mind*. But the term, mind, is not purely synonymous with soul. It is not adequate; and hence, its use as synonymous is not philosophically correct. Mind is the power or capability of purely intellectual action which is *possessed* by the soul. The soul, the principle of unity and permanency in the human compound, has the power of seeing with the eye, of hearing with the ear, and of exercising diverse actions with the other organs respectively. But it possesses, moreover, the power of *understanding*, the power of exercising cognitive action without employing any material instrument or bodily organ,—and this power we call intellect or *mind*. Mind is the general term for the power the soul possesses of exercising cognitive action without the use of an organ in the act. The soul possesses also another purely immaterial and spiritual power, the rational will. The discussion of the will, of the appetitive power, does not enter into our subject. We are occupied solely with the cognitive powers, with cognition.

Neither do we take up, at this point, the question of the soul. The discussion of the soul is in the domain of psychology. But we have had to speak of soul in order to indicate the root of unity in the human compound; and to divide off two sets of cognitive faculties possessed by the soul, the one whereby through the body it puts itself into communication with the world of matter, and the other whereby from material thus gained it builds up the structure of intellectual knowledge.

It is very easy to deny the existence of such a thing as a spiritual, immaterial soul and of immaterial thought, offering as a plea that they cannot be investigated by means of the eyes and the ears and the sense of touch. There is never any other ground upon which they are denied: but the denial of them on this ground always clearly indicates the lack of philosophical acumen and of philosophical education.

74. Acts of Intellect or Mind. The chief acts of the intellect are: 1, simple apprehension, that is, the forming of a concept or the catching of an idea; 2, judgment, which is the objective comparison of ideas and the consequent affirmation or denial of any given relationship between their objects as perceived; 3, reasoning or the comparison of the objective content of judgments, and the consequent affirmation or denial of new relationships perceived. The judgment, when finished, becomes practically an apprehension of a relation, thus giving a composite concept or idea; and the act of reasoning when finished gives us practically a complex idea or concept or notion.

For the defining of its concepts the intellect brings its activity into play under those phases which we call attention and abstraction. By means of attention it can concentrate itself upon one note or characteristic or quality in the object considered; and by the force of the will, even the outer sense may be made to subserve this concentration. Look, for instance, at any object. You get a visual perception, a sense perception of its color, figure, dimensions. Fix your attention on its color *only*, and you will find the eye following the mind and seeming not to notice the figure. Fix your attention on the figure, and you will find the eye apparently noticing not the color, but subserving the concentration of the mind upon the figure. We have here the beginning of *abstraction*—a thing so necessary in the formation of the idea—by which the mind abstracts from the total object perceived some one note, character or quality; and this abstraction is eventually carried so far that the mind neglects even the individuality of the color, figure, etc., as existing here and now in a particular object, and forms its universal idea of the given color or other quality as capable of being found concreted in many objects.

75. Mediate and Immediate Knowledge. Mediate knowledge is that which is obtained through the medium of the process of reasoning. We are not speaking here of knowledge obtained through the medium of human testimony. Immediate knowledge is that which is obtained without the medium of the process of reasoning. This immediate knowledge may regard either an individual fact gotten at by direct sense-perception, as "the sky is dark;" or it may regard a universal *a priori* principle such as "that which exists not cannot bring itself into existence." Immediate knowledge is obtained by what is called intuition, by merely *beholding* the truth. In reading certain philosophical works we must be on our guard not to be confused by the very indefinite way in which the term, *intuition*, is employed. It is well to give it one meaning, its real meaning, and to adhere tenaciously to that meaning: the beholding, perceiving, of a truth, whether individual fact or general principle, directly upon its presentation and without the aid of the reasoning process.

76. The Idea as a Sign. A very ancient expression employed in connection with the part which the idea plays in knowledge has been so extensively misused as to cause a very widespread error concerning the process of knowledge. The expression is this, "*signum quo*." It was in use when Latin was the universal language of the educated, and before any of the modern languages were even aspiring to a literature. The misunderstanding regarding the meaning of the expression has arisen from the manner in which it has been carried into our modern languages, that is by a mistake of translation. The idea *(idea)* was called a *signum quo objectum cognoscitur*, that is, a *sign by which the object is known*. But there are different kinds of signs. A sign is something that stands for something else. As we take the word *sign* in common discourse it means something by the perceiving of which we are led to think of something else. A sign may be a natural sign as being naturally connected with something else: thus smoke is a natural sign of fire. A sign may be purely arbitrary: thus the painted letters *Washington* indicate to us a great historic personality. These two kinds of signs are signs which *being seen first* lead us to think of that for which they stand. But when the idea was originally called a sign, *signum*, it was not so called in the sense that it was something that had first to be perceived so that from it we should be carried to think of something for which it stood. Remember that the idea is an act of the mind. Now this act is truly representative of something. But we do not first get an idea, then gaze mentally at that idea and out of the knowledge of it come to know the object of which it is representative and for which it stands. This would make knowledge an impossibility. For by perceiving the first idea we should simply get a second idea which would only be an idea or a sign of the first. We should have then to gaze mentally at this second idea to get a knowledge of the first. But what would happen then? We should simply get a third idea which would be a sign of the second. In gazing mentally at this we should get a fourth idea which would be a sign of the third. And thus through a lifetime we would not get through with one idea. What, then?

Two things must be kept in mind. The idea is a congnitive act; it is an act of the intellect; by it the object is known. But, moreover, just because it is a cognitive act it is in its entirety representative somehow of the object known. Since it is a cognitive act it is that by which (*quo*) we know the object; and since it is representative it can be called a sign (*signum*): so that thus it is really a sign by which (*signum quo*). But it is not a sign in the sense of the signs described above. It is a sign *in quo*, in which. In the very act we know the object; and it is called a sign simply because that cognitive act must be in its entirety representative. The other kind of sign, the smoke, for instance, is a sign *ex quo*, out of which, from which being known we know or infer the fire. The smoke as a sign has first to be known as an object, and from it we pass to the knowledge of another object, the fire. But we do not have to know the idea as a sign from which to infer the object of the idea; the idea is itself the act of knowledge. In fact, in an act of direct knowledge we do not advert to the idea. We advert to it only when by a reflex act of the mind we turn to the consideration of the idea as we would turn to the consideration of any other object of thought. Had the true original meaning of the idea as a sign been preserved, namely, that it is a *signum in quo* and not a *signum ex quo*, the philosophy of thought would have been spared many a charge of uncertainty and confusion.

77. The Universal Idea. Nominalism; Conceptualism; Realism. It is proper for us to call attention here to another confusion introduced into philosophy concerning the objective value of the idea that we denominate *universal*. In the book on Formal Logic (Laws of Thought, No. 19) we said, "When several objects are expressed by an idea, but in such a way that the idea not only embraces them all, but is applied to them distributively and individually, we have what is called a *universal* idea. Thus: *Man, horse, gold.* I can say, *Man is a living being*, meaning that *all men are living beings;* meaning also that each individual *man is a living being.* A plain exposition of what is meant by the universal idea, direct and reflex, will be found in the "Laws of Thought" (Nos. 20; 28). The special reason for introducing here once more, the subject of the Universal in so far as it is a matter of logic is, that the meaning of the expression has been confused by not a few writers who are given places of prominence. We may classify these writers as Nominalists, as Conceptualists and as Ultra-Realists.

Those whom we call Nominalists say that universality is only in the name, in terms, in words. Certainly, we do all admit a certain universality of signification attached to and belonging to words. But here, say the Nominalists, all universality of signification stops. When the term *man*, the word *man*, is used in the general sense, they say they can find no universal object *man in general* corresponding to it; hence, neither can there be any universal idea, because the idea is only representative of the object, and as there can be no such thing as a universal object so can there be no universal idea. It remains, therefore, according to them, that what is called universality of signification consists simply in the arbitrary use of one word or name to express a certain similitude which may have been perceived in various objects. Amongst Nominalists we might range Hobbes, Hume, Berkeley and J. S. Mill.

Conceptualists are those who, recognizing, of course, that there is a certain universality of meaning attached to words, add, very justly, that words are valueless except in so far as they are the faithful record and sign of ideas; and that, hence, whatever universality of signification attaches to the word or term, must necessarily attach to the idea or concept for which the word stands proxy, in the interchange of thought; nay that the universality accorded to the word—written or spoken—must necessarily belong primarily to the idea of which the word can never be more than an arbitrary representative appointed by the free will of the thinker. The Conceptualists, with the Nominalists, and alleging the same reason, deny all objective universality; but they assert that the universality of signification belongs primarily to the concept, and that it is only transferred arbitrarily to the word which happens to be chosen for the purpose of giving external expression to the concept. Kant's theory of knowledge is pure Conceptualism. Kant, not recognizing that we obtain true knowledge directly from objects, assumed that the intellect was supplied with a set of ideas which it applied to impressions received from without through the senses; that it instinctively applied the same idea (which he called "form,") to similar impressions, thus, in fact, building up the external world out of the mere idea. All "systems" of philosophy which begin by accepting Kant's assumption are easily reducible to Conceptualism.

The Ultra-Realist assumes that there is an actually existing universal something corresponding to the universal idea. The plea for Ultra-Realism we present briefly and with all its force as follows: It is agreed that an individual word can have a general or universal signification, the same word standing for the whole class and for all the objects of the class taken distributively. Now the Conceptualist has shown that this universality of signification in the word must necessarily belong, even previously, to the idea of which the word is only the appointed vicar. Following up his own line of argument the Conceptualist must logically admit that as even the idea itself is nothing more than the representative of the object, the intellectual vicar of the object, so, if there be a truly universal idea, there must also be a truly universal object of which the idea is only the intellectual representative. Thus, for example, besides the individual man known by the individual idea, there will be a universal something, a humanity-in-general-existing-as-one-object, represented by the general or universal idea, man. In so far as the theory of knowledge goes we may say that no writer of to-day thinks of directly advancing this ultra-realism. It was held by William of Champeaux in the twelfth century; and Aristotle, perhaps not too correctly, lays it to the account of Plato. Fundamentally, nevertheless, an ultra-realism is assumed by all writers of pantheistic tendencies.

What are we to hold? If we will be consistent we most hold to a certain realism. But if we will not reject experience, we must make this a realism that is not ultra. Nominalism and conceptualism both stop short of the truth; ultra-realism leaps beyond it.

We must avoid the defect and the excess. We must admit the signifying power which a word has to stand for many objects of a kind; and the same must be allowed to the concept, since the word is only the external expression of the concept. Yes, but term and concept are only the expression (oral and mental) of the object. Hence, the concept, whether individual or universal, must have its object. Hence we must say with the realist that not only the individual idea but also the universal idea has its object. However, we do not with the ultra-realist jump immediately to the conclusion that to the one idea of man in general, for instance, there corresponds a certain object which is man in general, in the same manner as an individual object, Christopher Columbus, corresponds to my individual idea. Here we part with the ultra-realist; and yet we remain realists, thus going beyond the nominalist and the conceptualist. Truth and consistency oblige us to hold to a certain realism which by some is denominated *moderate* to distinguish it from ultra-realism. What this object of the universal idea is, has been sufficiently explained for present purposes in that part of the "Laws of Thought" referred to above. The following example may perhaps serve to determine the meaning that is to be attached to the name realism or moderate realism.

Set yourself to thinking. Let your thoughts be these—"A triangle is a space enclosed by three straight lines; the three lines form three angles; the three angles added together will make 180° or two right angles; a line drawn parallel to one of the sides of the triangle and across the two other sides will divide these two other sides according to same ratio; etc., etc." What have you been doing? You have been using the concept or idea "triangle," in the universal sense; and, if you have been speaking your thoughts, you have been using the term "triangle" in the universal sense. You have been using idea and term in such a way as to embrace any and every triangle. Yet there is no such thing as a universal triangle existing or capable of existing in nature as the one object of this one idea or term which is universal in its application. We need not even claim that there is a triangle existing at all. Where, then, is the object of your universal idea? That is the question. The idea "triangle" which you have been using is applicable to any triangle whether actually existing or even only possible in the past, present or future—in eternity. Your idea is, therefore, fully universal. Nevertheless, it has not been directed to any one of them in particular. Whilst thinking, you did indeed use your imagination to picture to yourself some kind of a triangle. But this you did only as an aid to thought; and the picture was very vague and perhaps changing shape every few seconds, showing indifferently any sort of triangle-image, which, nevertheless, of whatever kind, was felt always to correspond to your idea of "triangle," this idea embracing simply the essentials common to any triangle possible in an eternity. What corresponded as an object to this idea? Not that ever changing image formed by the imagination, but a certain something which you threw out mentally before you as containing the essentials of the triangle and thus forming by a *fiction of the mind* an object which would stand you in the place of any and all triangles when you wished to think of triangle in general. This sort of object, the object of the universal idea, is called an *ens rationis*, a being of reason, since it is a creation of the intellect. Of course, as we have said, whilst you are thinking, the imagination will not be quiet but will keep on forming vague pictures of individual triangles; but these are not the object of the universal idea,—they are only material aids with which the imagination kindly supplies you whilst you are thinking. Now, here, in this object, this *ens rationis*, which the intellect fabricates for itself, we have, nevertheless, a realism. These essentials of triangle, collected from any triangle, are looked at as representative of the essence of any triangle whatsoever,—the individual peculiarities of said triangle and the individual triangle itself being thrown away and forgotten. The object is universal, as universal as the idea. Where does the realism lie? In this, that such object of the universal idea can be formed from any triangle in the possibilities, and that it can be applied to and stand for any triangle. The object, the fiction of the intellect, has its *ground in reality* wherever that reality does or even may exist. Though a creation of the mind, it is firmly grounded upon and legitimately formed from *any* and *all* the innumerable individual cases that do or may exist.

It is to be remarked of Nominalists that their universal term, and of Conceptualists, that their universal concept is not truly a universal. With very shallow philosophical insight they say that they simply *use* one word or concept to *stand* for many things in which a *similitude* is perceived. This absolutely destroys all claim to universality of signification in the term and concept; and it destroys, at a stroke, all science which is built upon *identity*, not upon *similitude* of signification, in the application of the terms that enter into general laws. Our universal idea has *one* object; this object relates to many; it can be formed, identically the same, from any one individual case; and its application back again to the individuals is not by way of similitude but by way of *identity*.

78. Thought. An idea is not commonly spoken of as thought; but as an element of thought. The term, thought, is usually presumed to imply predication, a judgment; and an idea is an element of the judgment. It is not even clear that we can have a solitary idea without simultaneously formulating some primary judgment in which it is contained either as subject or predicate. We have said a great deal about the universal idea because it is an absolutely essential element in continuous thought. If we had no universal ideas, our thoughts, our judgments would follow one another simply like shooting stars, each and every judgment reducing itself to an individual affirmation. Each judgment would reduce itself to the formula "this is this" and could not pass beyond. We could not so much as say, *water is liquid*, because we should thus be using the subject in the universal sense. If there were not universal ideas it would not be lawful for us to combine the thing here present to us with other things absent or possible which we would designate by the same term, water. And in applying the designation, water, to the present thing under consideration we should have to apply it individually as we apply the name George Washington to a one something. After applying the name, water, to one thing, with which we slaked our thirst by the roadside, it would be absurd to apply the same name, water, to another thing near by in which we washed our hands, unless we admitted the universal both in the idea and in the term. If there were no universal idea combining even these two in an identical intellectual representation it would still be more ridiculous, when words are so easily made, to employ the same word, water, ten thousand times over, to characterize as many separate liquid things met with in the course of a life-time. Then, the same difficulty arises with regard to the use of the term, liquid, in the various judgments. Have we or have we not a general notion, which we express by the term, liquid? If we have not, why should we create such confusion by employing the same word to express so many things? But if there is no universality of ideas, what do all judgments become? Merely "this is this" and "that is that," and science is brought down to a list of predications regarding each individual thing that can be thought of. Science can be no longer a simultaneous predication for all the individuals of a class. The science of gravitation must be expanded to a list of predications separate and distinct for each individual atom of matter.

We have here, then, clearly enough manifested to us by the very needs of life the objective value of the universal judgment. The truth of thought consists in the correspondence of thought—in its own native representative way—to object. By object is meant not merely that which is the object of sense-perception. Object means *whatsoever* can be thought of, whether it be in itself perceptible to sense or not. Thought itself can be made an actual object of thought; and such we are making it in our present consideration. Thought, judgment, must necessarily correspond to object when we make no declaration beyond what is objectively presented to us.

Is argument thought? Yes. Is there argument in the object or objects reasoned about? No. How, then, does argument correspond to object? In this way. Argument is nothing else than the natural human mental method of acquiring knowledge, in which the universal idea is used as a stepping stone from one judgment to another. Each individual premiss, major and minor (excluding the case of error), has its own correspondence. The premisses are, equivalently at least, a composite apprehension, in which a common notion is perceived to be, objectively, either identified with each of two other notions, or, identified with one of them and excluded by the other. The two judgments are thus, therefore, treated as a composite of ideas and are put together to form a new judgment just as two simple ideas would be combined in a simple judgment. When the two judgments are approached to one another and are seen by means of the common part, which is represented by the middle term, to merge into one, objectively, the result perceived is expressed by the affirmative conclusion, which is the mental expression of what has been thus objectively perceived just as clearly and as surely as in the simple judgment; but if only one of the notions is seen to be identified objectively with the notion expressed by the middle term, whilst the other is excluded by it, the result perceived is expressed by the negative conclusion.

CHAPTER XII. ERROR.

Error—Error is not Physically Necessary—The Savage and the Sun—Error and the Will—Error and Opinion—Normal State—Objections Raised—An Idealist Difficulty.

79. Error. What was said of logical truth is to be said of logical falsity or error, namely, that it is to be found in the strictly defined judgment, only; in the mental act which associates two objects of apprehension by affirmative predication or dissociates them by negative predication; in the act which affirms or denies. There can be no error in the simple apprehension or in the sense-perception. For as we cannot apprehend what does not come before the mind for apprehension, nor see, for instance, what is not presented to the eye to be seen, there is no possibility of error being committed in the execution of these acts.

We do, indeed, often hear and read the expressions, "false ideas," "false notions;" but there cannot be a false idea or notion, because the idea or notion, though an element-of-the-judgment, must be considered as simply an element and as independent of all affirmation or denial. The expressions "false ideas," "false notions," are, then, really intended to indicate false judgments, false definitions, which have been unwarily accepted. Thus, when a man is said to have a false idea of justice, or honor, or education, what is meant is, that he has accepted a false definition of justice or honor or education, that he has formed a false judgment, that he has coupled with the idea of justice or of honor or of education other ideas which do not belong to it at all or which do not belong to it in the way in which he has judged.

80. Error is not Physically Necessary. Error, then, attaches to the judgment. It is the non-conformity of the judgment with the object upon which the judgment in its representative character passes sentence. But here arises a difficulty. The act of judgment is the perception or affirmation, or if you will, the perception *and* affirmation of the objective agreement or disagreement of two concepts. When there is an error, the judgment does not conform to the object. But, how can this be? The intellect perceives simply that which is presented to it. How, then, can it affirm that which is not presented to it, and hold to this affirmation as though it had perceived what it affirms? How can it commit an error? The intellect, certainly, cannot choose to perceive that which is not presented to it; neither can it be forced to such act of perception. For, such act is an impossibility. By the physical law of its nature the intellect is necessitated to the perception of that, and of that only, which is presented to it with evidence, just as by a physical law the eye, in good condition, must see by the light and cannot see by darkness, and just as matter must gravitate towards matter and cannot tend from matter. Hence, should we admit that error could be, in any instance, physically necessary, this could be only on the ground that a truth presented to the intellect should shine not with its own evidence but with the evidence of some other truth, even of its own contradictory. How, then, can an error be caused? What is its origin or source? Error, we have said, is the non-conformity of the affirmation or negation with the object. But this cannot come from the object; because the object has nothing but its own evidence to present. It cannot come from the natural activity which the intellect exercises of itself; because the intellect by itself simply accepts the evidence and reproduces mentally the objective truth. The cause of the non-conformity is to be found elsewhere. It is to be found in the will. Whenever there is an error, there are two judgments. There is the natural act of the intellect by which a certain evidence is received and a certain objective truth is affirmed; and besides this, there is a pure affirmation made under the impulse of the will beyond the evidence and, therefore, without evidence. Let us try to explain this by an example.

81. The Savage and the Sun. A savage sits all day at the door of his hut looking towards the south. In the morning he sees the sun to his left and low upon the horizon. In the middle of the day it is above him. Just before the night sets in it is again low upon the horizon, but to his right. What is really evident to the savage? One thing; a change in the relative positions of himself and the sun. What might be the cause of this phenomenon, to-wit, the evident change of relative positions? It might be movement on the part of the sun. It might be movement on the part of the savage and his hut. It might be movement of both the savage and the sun. There is evidence to the savage of a change of relative positions. By the physical law of his intellect he has to receive this evidence; and in the act of thus receiving it, passes his infallible judgment upon the relative change. But perhaps he does more. It may be that he goes beyond the evidence. Whilst he has been sitting at the door of his hut he has seen the flight of birds across the sky, and he has seen the path of the arrows which his fellow savages sent after the birds. He did not move; but the birds did, and so did the arrows. There was a change of relative position between himself on the one hand, and the birds and arrows on the other; and the cause of this phenomenon presented to him with evidence was the movement of the birds and of the arrows. He has found an actual cause in one case. It would be a sufficient cause in the other case. He goes no further, but affirms: the sun moves around the earth. This is a pure affirmation, a mock judgment made without evidence under the impulse of the will. There is evidence, indeed, that this *would* be a *sufficient* cause; but there is not evidence that this is *the* cause. However, the natural inquisitiveness of the intellect being satisfied, the will interferes and orders to be taken for granted this false declaration which quiets the tendency of the savage intellect. Under the same impulse the savage might declare the moon to be flat.

We can secure plentiful parallel illustrations without going to the extremity of providing ourselves with a savage.

82. Error and the Will. Error, then, always implies an act of will at its source. It is the acceptance of a false declaration which is not forced by evidence, since there is no evidence. The acceptance, therefore, not being spontaneous, that is, necessitated by the very nature of the intellect, must be brought about by the will. There is an element of will entering somewhere; there is some good perceived which motives the will to the acceptance of the declaration as satisfactory. The erroneous declaration satisfies some present craving of the human person. It satisfies some appetency which happens to be manifesting itself. The appetency may be of the speculative or of the practical order. It may be a thirst for knowledge in the way of sufficient causes; or it may be a longing to which there is held out a hope of being satisfied through a conclusion drawn without a consideration of many modifying circumstances. There is, indeed, just enough to calm the present tendency. The will steps in: it stops the investigation. For, the will is a blind power; it does not see for itself: and the craving is clamoring against delay. Or, the will, under the same restless demand, even turns the intellect to the contemplation of favoring analogies and of arguments which in their incompleteness make for the justice of the desired end. Under the impulse of the will, then, the attention of the intellect may be arrested or it may be so directed as to be given no chance for reflex consideration, the will forcing it here and there to skip an evidence and to take in any plausible appearance that may suit the present emotion. The vehemence of the appetition by which the will is moved may be re-enforced by special conditions on the part of the intellect; by prejudices, incautious acceptance of testimony, forgetfulness, confusion of previously received knowledge and of the meaning of terms, by want of capacity, etc.

It would be difficult, and it is certainly out of place here to attempt to enumerate the thousand inclinations, the bewildering complexities of motives that lie at the root of erroneous judgments. We may be simply in a hurry, and we leap at conclusions. We may, perhaps, be a little lazy, and only too glad to shirk the searching investigation. How readily this may happen in things which are not of vital importance! With the knowledge we have gained by experience of the general correctness of certain judgments made upon certain data, we plough ahead through decisions for the sake of gaining time and saving labor.

Sometimes, when a correct conclusion can be drawn no otherwise than by the combination of the evidences of numerous data and there happens to be a lack of memory or instruction or a lack of skill in composing the various evidences, vanity and presumption may strongly solicit the will to the acceptance of a false declaration.

New evidences of further truths are always presenting themselves to the mind as education advances. At the same time, by graduated practice, constantly increasing skill is acquired for the combination of evidences in complicated processes. An excellent illustration of this and of the possibilities of error may be found in the progress of a game of chess. Both players have the game entirely open before them. The beginner does not see the distant complication that is evident to the expert. And even if both players are equally matched, it may be that whilst one is announcing his own victory in the next move,—he is mated by his opponent.

Although, as we have said, error can never be a physical necessity, since this would imply the beholding of evidence where there is no evidence, still error may sometimes be morally inevitable. When we say that error is morally inevitable or morally necessary, we mean, that, considering the way in which men *do* (not *must*) use their free will, we may rest satisfied that in given circumstances they *will* (not *must*) use it in such a way as to accept a false declaration. It is on a clever application of this principle that the success of the marvellous tricks of jugglers is based. It is morally impossible that the savage should not accept with the quiet of certitude his decision in regard to the movement of the sun. Nothing had ever been said to him and no thought had ever occurred to him which might lead him to suspect the rotation of the earth. He thought of but one sufficient explanation for the phenomenon of change of position. This explanation was a movement on the part of the sun. He accepted his conclusion as a manifest application of a principle which he had drawn by induction from his life's experience. His error was a moral necessity.

83. Error and Opinion. We must be careful not to confound opinion with error. The adhering to an opinion merely as an opinion, is not an error, even though the opinion be what we call the wrong opinion. Of two contradictory statements, one person may hold the one as an opinion, and another the other. This means only that the arguments for one statement seem the more weighty to the first person, and that the arguments for the other statement seem the more weighty to the second person. One of the statements is undoubtedly false; yet neither is evidently so.

The quite general acceptance of an opinion does not indicate that it is held with certitude nor that its contradictory is denied. It is held as very highly probable; and its contradictory, as hardly or very slightly probable. Though a very highly probable opinion does not rise to the degree of certitude, still men will often act upon it without hesitation, recognizing all the time that it is only an opinion; and indeed many of the benefits of civilization owe their wide extension much to the fact that in the material affairs of life men are often content to act upon a very strong probability.

84. Normal State. We have to repeat here, once more, that we are speaking of the normal man—of man in what is recognized to be the normal state of the human body. The organ of hearing may be so affected that there is no perception of sound; and the organ of vision, so that there is no visual response to the emission of light-rays from external objects. The sensory nerves may be in such condition that what we call contact-perception by touch ceases absolutely to manifest itself. But these are not normal states.

Hence, in discussing the general principles of cognition in the normal man, we are not obliged to introduce the discussion of the various abnormal conditions of the nervous organism. Taking this necessary stand—necessary that we may be able to speak of the human race in general,—we rid ourselves at once of a thousand and one objections which are to no purpose but which can be brought in at inopportune moments to arrest the progress of our study. The man born blind will form judgments of color as of something that can be reached by touch; and the man born deaf will form judgments of sound as of something that can be reached by sight. Of course, the error, here, starts in the will urging the intellect to strive after a vague concept, and the judgment is formed, under the impetus of the thirst for knowledge, without sufficient grounds. The same is to be said of all false judgments formed upon sense-perceptions made through organs partially deranged. Therefore, all cases out of the normal, as well where the perceptive organism is partially deranged as where it is totally and hopelessly disordered in any particular, are outside of the general discussion entirely.

Those who have what are termed hallucinations, who seem, for example, to see what they do not see, or to hear sounds that do not exist, are to be classed with the hopelessly disordered, so long as these hallucinations exist. That their perceptive organism is affected under the hallucination in the same manner as when there is real perception with an object perceived cannot be denied, as we may learn from those who suffer in this way and who recognize, afterwards, that they have been under the hallucination. Once they become cognizant of their affection they may, by suspending judgment for a while in particular matters, do much to avoid false judgments. But the case of the erroneous judgment made in good faith under the hallucination does not belong to the normal human condition which we are considering. It is a case where by the influence of some particular disease the sensory organ is modified from within just as it would have been modified from without in normal sense-perception.

85. Objections Raised. The great objection raised against the truth of mere perception is that even when the organs are normal, the appearance in many cases is always contrary to the fact. This objection is brought particularly against the trustworthiness of perception by vision. What we have already said about vision will be remembered. The eye does not see distance except as on a plane perpendicular to the axis of vision. The eye merely receives variations of light and shade (of brighter and darker) in color, which are separated from one another only as on such a plane. Hence the impression of the landscape is no other than it would be if the same lights and shades in color came from the flat surface of the canvas; and these lights and shades are sometimes reproduced upon the canvas with such imitative skill that the imitation cannot be distinguished from the reality.

A special difficulty may be that of the direction of lines even on the perpendicular plane. You are sitting in a small boat which rests upon the bosom of a clear lake. The oars are hanging idle in the water. You look down, and lo! the oar seems to bend at the water's edge. And yet it is not bent. Here is a presentation that differs from the reality. Not at all. You are receiving light rays from an object (the part of the oar under water) through two mediums of different densities, the water and the atmosphere. The light rays change direction when passing from one medium to the other. If you want to pass judgment upon the straightness of the oar you must take the fact of refraction into consideration. Again, you are travelling over the prairie on a train. The rails run out behind you in straight parallel lines. You know that the rails are parallel, because the train has run over them safely. Yet they are presented to the eye as coming together in the distance. The presentation contradicts the fact! In no wise. You must see and judge according to the law of vision. Sight will not give you everything. Sight will not give you the odor of the violet. In the case of the rails you are not making account of what is known as the angle of vision. Take a rod as long as the width of the rails, say six feet. Hold it up before you a foot away and parallel to the line running through the two eyes. The rod will cross the whole field of vision. Let the rod be carried away from you, and you will find that it crosses less and less of the field of vision as the angle of vision decreases. When the rod is at the point where the rails seemed to meet, it will not seem to cover more than that one point. All this is to be taken into account; it is the law of vision. If you are not satisfied at having the vanishing point so near to you, provide yourself with a telescope.

Another difficulty sometimes presented is this, that in the physical sciences a law may be held for a while as certain, and then be rejected as false. What reliance can be placed upon the value of the second, even contradictory, law that has been substituted in its place? Witness the belief through ages of the Ptolemaic assertion that the sun revolved around the earth. With regard to theories in the natural sciences, this is to be said in general: We must remember that they are theories and that they are to be held only as theories. As theories they are always on trial. With regard to Ptolemy's assumption, we must know that it was never undisputed. But for working purposes it served the astronomer to assume that the sun moved around the earth. His calculations were made longer in many cases; but, in many other cases, they were made shorter than they would have been upon the now accepted fact that the earth moves around the sun. We must always be cautious about theories. When that which is only theory is laid down and upheld as certain and ascertained law (a thing that happens too often to-day with regard to geological and archeological theories) the error in ninety-nine instances out of the hundred is one of presumption; it is an error starting in the will which is moved by the vanity usually found close upon the heels of superficial knowledge. It is only an illustration of the old saw, that a little knowledge is a dangerous thing.

86. An Idealist Difficulty. The one really great difficulty which the idealistic or theoretic sceptic proposes to himself and in face of which, as something impassable, he begins to build up his theories of idealism, is this: he does not see how the mind can possess the outer world without going out of itself—a thing which the mind certainly cannot do. He seems to talk of the mind and the object as of a gun and a target. When we say that the gun has hit the target we mean that a projectile has gone from the gun to the target. Similarly, the idealist would seem to imply or conclude that when we say that the mind apprehends an external object distinct from itself, we mean that the mind goes out to seize upon the object: and as he does not find this strange circumstance in his experience, he is content to deny the true objectivity of knowledge. Thus he lays down an unfounded theory as the only explanation for a fact (the fact of the knowledge of external reality), and as experience will not support the unfounded theory he contents himself with a denial of the fact. If he would but admit in theory, as he does in practice for very life's sake, and as he should do in theory to have his theory of consciousness consistent,—if he would but recognize his own experience, which is that of mankind, that the outer object stimulates the animated organ and that this organ is animated by the principle of life (the same principle that sees by the aid of the eye as it grasps by the aid of the hand and perceives its own thought), he would have no difficulty. Of course your mind cannot make an excursion away out to the planet Jupiter; neither can the great planet with all his satellites come right into your eye. The senses are, as it were, so many living doors at which the outer world of matter knocks, so to say, for admission into the realm of knowledge without going in itself, and through which, we, thus wakened to the demand, stretch forth to the object outside and possess it by knowledge without going out ourselves. When the landscape projects itself upon the retina and we turn the eyes to give every detail the best opportunity to present its individual petition to be known, the landscape does not enter the power of vision, nor does the power of vision go out to the object. The object and the power meet, so to say, half way. Consciousness is wakened in the modification of the living organism. In that wakening the object becomes sufficiently present; and, through what takes place in the modification of the organism and the wakening of consciousness, the knowing power seizes the outer object at once in knowledge. Take an illustration from the work of the camera—though no illustration is the true counterpart of that which it is intended to illustrate. There is a picture outside, and there is a sensitized plate inside. The light-rays work their way through the lenses and are caught on the sensitized plate within. Suppose the camera to be a living thing, and the lenses and the plate to be its visual organ,—what happens? The visual power is simply directed along the lines of the light-rays as to something outside. In the power of sight in man there is a real living plate, the retina, which is a part of the man. It does not, like the plate which we call "sensitized," catch a dead image. But the living spirit which animates, vivifies, the organ, cognizes the variations of brightness and shade and color,—directing itself out along the line of the rays. It cognizes the individual picture, and with its recuperative capacity, it washes away the picture so soon as the object is gone; but it has stored up the picture in memory and it has universalized it in the idea. There is simply a result. That result is knowledge. That the object has something to do in the process, I know; for I can close my eyes and oppose to its entrance an impenetrable wall of exclusion. The outward material object has efficiency as a real cause to put the organ of perception into the state required for the perceptive act. To deny this is to deny the very principle of causality; and to deny the principle of causality is to land oneself in absolute scepticism.

To refer again to the number of the senses, the ancient division into five is sufficient for us in this treatise on the general truth of thought. Should we possibly discover a new sense whose work we have been crediting to one of the five, such discovery would be but the most powerful confirmation of all that we have been saying; it would show that the physical laws of human nature had been regularly executed and that sense-perception had been exercised in spite of the much or the little that we knew about it. Such discovery would only corroborate the truth, that by those very physical laws of human nature the human person takes possession, by knowledge, of the outer world with the same necessity and spontaneity that accompany the conscious recognition of the inner thing of thought and the existence of self; that there exists in man for the perception of the material non-ego the same natural fitness which he possesses for the perception of the ego and its modifications, and that the two perceptions are performed with the same ease and security. As we have previously noted, if only the same reflection be made upon self perceiving the outer world that is made upon self thinking the inner thought, it will be seen that there is the same testimony in the conscious self for the existence of matter as for the existence of mind. The idealist or the agnostic sceptic cannot appeal, for the reality of his thought or what he may choose to call his state of consciousness, to anything which will not serve as an equally valid testimony for the reality of the outer world which is reached by sense-perception.

CHAPTER XIII. CRITERION AND EVIDENCE.

The Word, Criterion—Some Answers—Evidence—Descartes and Reid—Objective Truth—The Word, Evidence—Evidence: Immediate and Mediate; Intrinsic and Extrinsic—The Beginnings of Knowledge.

87. The Word, Criterion. A criterion, (κριτήριον) is a standard by which to judge (κρίνειν). We speak here of the criterion of logical truth, of the standard by which to test the representative value of a given judgment. Is this, my judgment, a true judgment? If so, why? How do I know that it is true? In assigning a reason, I will, at once, say that I have seen, heard, understood, etc., mentioning one or another perceptive act according to the peculiar subject-matter of the judgment in question. Thus, I appeal to the veracity of the various cognitive faculties. I appeal to their testimony, which I hold to be worthy of trust, as to a test, a standard. I thus admit the fact of *a* criterion, in the physically necessary truthfulness of the perceptive faculties. But the question presents itself: in each of these cases and in similar cases, is there an assignable reason beyond? What is the final reason, the final criterion in each case? And then another question presents itself: is the final reason the same in all cases? Is there a final or ultimate criterion which is also universal? Is there one final universal basis for certitude? one final test to which we must appeal in all cases and beyond which there is no appeal?

Is there one universal and ultimate criterion, and if there be, what is it? The answer is a very simple one, indeed. Yet the very simplicity of the answer has made the question a puzzling one to philosophers. We must necessarily meet here the same difficulties that are encountered in every question concerning knowledge when one presumes to inquire beyond the limits of inquiry, that is, beyond the limits of immediate evidence. The criterion must be in the judgment itself or outside of the judgment. If it be outside of the judgment or mental act to be tested, it will be either in the particular objective truth of which we are judging or it will be somewhere else.

88. Some Answers. All pure idealists put the criterion in the subject thinking. For, they hold that knowledge comes from within; and thus they are forced to appeal to the thought itself for whatever value they may wish to give to it.

The Traditionalists, for whose doctrine we may signalize De Lamennais (1782-1854; *Essai sur l'indifférence*) as the modern exponent, say that the final criterion is outside-authority. De Lamennais, affirming a primitive revelation of truth to the human race, contends that this truth has passed down from generation to generation; and that the ultimate criterion of truth and of certitude can thus be nothing else than the authority of the human race manifested by the general consent of mankind. It is easy to see that the authority of all men existing at a given period could not be used as a criterion: for what life-time would suffice to take the testimony of all men on a single question? We shall allow him, then, to mean the testimony of the majority of men. But neither could this be a criterion for us; since, were we obliged to appeal to the majority of men for the certification of but half a dozen acts of knowledge, we should be landed in utter scepticism—such an appeal being an impossibilty.

Blind instinct is sometimes advanced as the ultimate criterion. We are conscious that we are forced to believe, it is said, and there we must stop all inquiry. But we cannot take blind instinct for a last criterion. We cannot appeal to it for the reality of objective truth. Such a criterion would lead us to the Kantian dogma that knowledge comes out of the mind and not into it. It would, moreover, reduce us eventually to a blind scepticism, allowing us to affirm no objective reality with reason. The fact of the blind instinct would have to be affirmed by another movement of the blind instinct; and so on indefinitely. The holding of this criterion has been ascribed to Thomas Reid and the Scottish school. But whatever the Scottish philosophers may have written, we believe they did not intend to hold to this as the ultimate criterion. We shall have a word to say about them later on.

The sentimentalists, with J. J. Rousseau, say that the ultimate criterion is mere feeling. This has all the difficulties of the preceding. It does not certify the reality of the object. And, besides, it makes certitude a very uncertain thing, changeable regarding the same thing with every changing mood. As a criterion, it is characteristic of the sceptical school which advocates it. It allows room for a denial of everything according to the mood of the hour, and, at the same time, affords a specious pretext for the admissions which the sceptic is obliged to make when he lives amongst men.

We place the ultimate criterion in the object, in the objective truth upon which judgment is passed. What we mean by this we shall endeavor to make plain in the following number. Understand, first, that we are asserting a criterion for every kind of judgment, the analytic and the synthetic, the universal, the particular, and the singular. Be the judgment what you will,—"That field is green," "Parallel lines always remain at the same distance from one another," etc., the criterion will be ever the same: *objective evidence*.

89. Evidence. Understand well where the great difficulty lies. It lies in this: in deciding whether, for the determination of the truth of a judgment and of the motive of our firm adherence to it, we are to rest in the clearness of the judgment itself, or whether we are to make an appeal to the objective truth enunciated by the judgment. The force of the difficulty will manifest itself as we proceed. We are here at the last issue of philosophy. Perhaps some examples may enable us to understand a very fundamental truth which many have failed to recognize by reason of its most patent simplicity.

You are seated by the window with a friend; and there is a plant upon the sill. As you look out you form in your mind the following judgment: "That rose is red." You then give expression to your judgment in words. But, a moment later, whilst you are about to turn your attention to some pictures in your hand, you begin to doubt the truth of the judgment you have just made, or, your friend calls its truth in question. What do you do to settle your own doubt, or, if you have no doubt, what test for the correctness of your judgment do you offer to the one who has contradicted your assertion? You appeal to the object; and you require your friend to do the same. You look *again at the object;* and you request him to *look again at the object.* You and your friend do not merely close your eyes and appeal to the judgments you have formed. But what does this mean practically? It means that neither of you expects to find in the judgment itself the test of the truth of the judgment. Each one of you goes to the object for the test, for the *Criterion.* That which you expect to find in the object is the *objective-shining-out-of-the-truth*, which you accept as the final test of the correctness of your subjective expression, of your judgment. If the judgment happened to have been made upon a passing object which has ceased to be present, you will have to appeal as well as you can to memory.. But how will you appeal to memory? You will not appeal to the mere judgment or enunciation as it remains in the memory; but you will appeal to the image of the rose and its color, as these are *objects* of the memory and imagination.

Suppose, again, that you were to find a person who was laboring under an hallucination of vision and who professed to see something which was not present—what would you do, what final method would you adopt, to convince him of his error? Would you ask him to appeal to something subjective, to that erroneous judgment which he has already formed? No, you would recognize the utter futility of such appeal. You would try to discover some way of making him apply to the object. You would invite him to try the test of touch upon the supposed object. And what does this signify to our present purpose? It signifies that you recognize the criterion to be something objective and not subjective.

It may be retorted that we are here appealing to something purely subjective, since the sensation of touch is purely subjective. Yes; in its individual entity as an act, not only the sensation of touch, but the sensation of vision and every other sensation is purely subjective. That is to say, it belongs to you as subject perceiving. If it were not thus purely subjective, that is, altogether in you, you could not claim it as entirely your sensation. But consider what is implied in a sensation and in the judgment accompanying or following. Every perceptive act is a subjective modification or mood. This mood is an utterance, a declaration of the existence of something which is not the mood itself. The mood, thus, as an utterance, is relative. It is of its value as relative that there is question here. To discover this, you must go to the term of the relation, to the object which is referred to, which is declared.

Once more: in making the test of a judgment, you always repeat the judgment. But you do not merely repeat the declaration as you find it in your mind. You repeat the whole process: you go through all the conditions necessary for the original forming of the judgment. One of these original conditions is always that the power be put in communication with the object. Why do you put the power in communication with the object? To see if the power will be forced to render the verdict, to see if the same testimony will be wrung from it. By what? By the inevitable light with which truth is illumined, and whereby it coerces the faculty to its recognition. This power which truth possesses by reason of its own light and whereby it forces its representation upon the vital faculty is called its evidence. This is objective and cannot be subjective; for it is the shining of the truth in its own light.

There are some who are ready to quibble here, saying that the criterion is the evidence as perceived; but, that, the perceiving is something entirely subjective; and that, hence, the criterion must in the end be regarded as subjective. This is a sophism. We have been showing how the search for the general or universal criterion of logical truth must lead us ultimately to the evidence of the objective truth, to something outside of the faculty. Now if you take up any particular, concrete judgment, or act of knowledge, will the criterion be the evidence as perceived? Certainly, it will be the evidence *as perceived;* but the evidence is perceived *as objective*, not *as subjective*. Objectivity of truth is the condition *sine qua non* of the act of judgment; and objectivity of the evidence of that truth is the final formality to which we must have recourse to test the truth of the act of judgment, the truth of thought.

Sometimes we find evidence distinguished into objective and subjective; by objective evidence is meant that of which we have just spoken and which we shall term "evidence" without any qualification; by subjective evidence is meant the corresponding clearness and distinctness in the judgment passed. But evidence belongs to object; and not to intellect as expressing object. It is important that we should hold to this application of the term;—and we lay stress upon it as we laid stress upon the necessity of limiting the term, certitude, to the state of the mind and of not transferring it to the object. It is I who am certain, it is I who have certitude; it is the object which is evident.

90. Descartes and Reid. Descartes tried vainly to work out a complete theory of the process and progress of knowledge and of certitude on the basis of a fundamental truth, the conviction, the affirmation and acceptance of which he found inevitable, when all else had been called into doubt. This truth was the fact of his own thought, which he expressed in the judgment, "*ego cogito*"—I think. But the last, the ultimate motive which he assigns for certitude in this declaration, is the "clear and distinct perception" he has of that thinking ego.

Though the writings of Descartes are certainly very incoherent and very ambiguous whenever he touches this question, we should be pleased to be able to profit by his ambiguity for the sake of interpreting him as being in accord with rather than in opposition to the mind of humanity. But explain him as we will, we find him always escaping us and retrenching himself in the idea as his last security for the assertion of objective reality.

When we say that the last criterion cannot be subjective, the term *subjective* applies to the particular act of judgment made; and we mean that the particular act of judgment cannot be taken as the ultimate basis of certitude regarding the object upon which the judgment is passed. Your existence, your self, your thought, your feelings are certainly subjective to *you*. But they are all objective, object, to your perception of them and to your judgment passed upon them. Now, if we follow Descartes down through all his doubts, and doubts of doubts, to the point where he finds himself at a primary fact of which he feels he cannot doubt, the fact of self thinking, upon which he pronounces the judgment "I think;" we see plainly that he is making the doubting or thinking ego the object of a second perception or judgment in which he declares "I think." Had he recognized here that the motive of this declaration was the evidence of the thinking ego which presented itself as object to the second or reflex perception, he might have found his way back to reality. Instead of doing this he turns to the second or reflex mental act to seek therein a "clear and distinct perception" of the original thinking ego taken as object. Now, who is there who does not see that for the perception of this "clear and distinct perception" in the second act there is required a third mental act? But is the third mental act reliable? Yes; if it contains a "clear and distinct perception" of the other "clear and distinct perception." How shall we know this? By making it the object of a fourth mental act. Thus we are led farther and farther away from objective reality deep into the depths of idealistic reflection. Descartes, in his attempt at an explanation, is perpetually appealing to the true criterion, the evidence of the object and the objective truth; and by his confusion of terms he forces us to conclude that he had not a very "clear and distinct idea" of his own profound secret.

The Scottish school of philosophy, of which we may regard Thomas Reid as the proper exponent, has been charged with making the *sensus communis* (the general and uniform consent of the human race) the court of appeal for truth and certitude, to the extent that when we question the authority of this court we are thrown back upon the blind instinct of men to believe. As for the keen Scottish philosophers, we should find it difficult to class them as a school, since they differ so widely on very essential points. But concerning the matter here in question we shall say that they spent so much time in searching for and classifying those fundamental truths universally accepted by men, that they failed to investigate to its depths the basis of this acceptance. Of course, universal acceptance is *a* criterion beyond which we need not go to feel secure in certain judgments that regard the necessities of human life and action. But it is not a universal nor an ultimate criterion. In his printed works Reid does style it an ultimate criterion; and by his printed works is he judged in critical philosophy. But it is pleasant to note that in manuscripts still extant Reid makes the following declaration: "Evidence is the sole and ultimate ground of belief, and self-evidence is the strongest possible ground of belief, and he who desires reason for believing what is self-evident knows not what he means." * Studying the mind of writers and not merely random declarations scattered through their printed works, we believe that both Reid and Stewart put the criterion where it ought to be, in evidence.

91. Objective Truth. We have said that there may be many criteria of truth or, what comes to the same, many motives of certitude. I may be set at rest by the testimony of my own eyes, by the relation of a friend, by a document, by an argument, etc. But we have, here, been looking for a last reason, a last resort, which will be the same in every investigation, when we go on asking why, why, why. This last resort, we have seen, will be the evidence of the objective truth. Attention is called once more, and separately, to the meaning of the expression, objective truth. By objective truth we mean any fact or principle which is known or can be known. Even the act by which said fact or principle is known can become objective truth with reference to another act of knowing. Whatever there may be which will not imply contradiction in its statement, be it abstract

*(Dr. James McCosh, *The Scottish Philosophy*, citing from manuscripts of Reid in the possession of Francis Esmond).

principle; be it concrete fact, past, present or future; or neither abstract principle nor fact that was or will be, but only a mere possibility that shall never be realized but is only conceivable as not involving a contradiction in itself;—all this is included in the expression, objective truth.

Whatever is knowable, in so far as it is knowable, does, by the fact that it is knowable, present itself in its character of knowable when it is encountered by a knowing power which is adequate to the perception of the peculiar knowability presented. This capability in the knowable, in the objective truth, of presenting itself, we have called its evidence. The act of self-presentation cannot be exercised by every objective truth in reference to every knowing power. Linear measure cannot present itself as such to hearing. The harmony of a musical chord cannot present itself as such to touch. Odor cannot present itself to vision. The truth that parallel lines produced will never meet, cannot present itself to taste. But sound can present itself for perception to hearing; and linear measure can present itself to be perceived by sight and touch.

92. The Word, Evidence. Evidence is the shining of the truth in its own light; it is the necessary visibility of the truth. It will be noticed that the words, evidence, shining, light, visibility, are all taken from what belongs to the visible and to the power of perceptibility by vision. So wonderful a part does sight play in perception as a vital matter in the economy of human life, that we come to use the word *see* for every kind of perception. We say that we see how justice is a virtue: but we do not see it, we understand it by the perception of the intellect. We are told that one of the voices in a quartette is false; and, for proof, we are told to wait until the quartette sings—and we shall *see*. In this case *see* is used instead of *hear*. We use it also for taste: "You do not know the taste of the strawberry? No? Well, take this and *see!*" Thus we employ the word, see, to express every kind of perception; and we also transfer the words that relate to vision, to express like relations of other kinds of perception. This is what happens with the words, evidence and evident. Evident *(evidens)* and evidence *(evidentia)* are from the Latin *e-videre*, to see out of. A thing is evident when it is seen out of (out from) itself. Evidence is the capacity a thing has to be seen out of itself, by itself, from itself. So, whatever presents itself—be it fact, principle, possibility or argument—whatever presents itself to any knowing power so as to be perceived by that knowing power, is said to be evident to that knowing power; and it is perceivable by reason of its evidence which is its ability to present itself for cognition to the knowing power that is adapted to the perception of it.

93. Evidence: Immediate and Mediate: Intrinsic and Extrinsic. A truth is said to be immediately evident when it is perceptible directly in its own evidence without the medium of the evidence of other truths to make it perceptible. Thus we can have immediate evidence of contingent truths, such as, that a fire which is close to us is warm, or, that one of two lines is shorter than the other; and we have immediate evidence of certain general analytic truths, as, that parallel lines produced do not meet. But when a truth requires the medium of the evidence of another truth to make itself perceptible, its evidence is said to be mediate. Thus we may not be able to see which of two lines is the longer, but by the medium of a movable measure we shall discover it very readily. The evidence of a truth which we arrive at only through argument, that is, the evidence of a conclusion, is mediate; it is perceived by means of the light that is thrown upon it by the evidence of the premisses.

I would call attention, here, to the meaning of the word *proof*. It is said very justly that in philosophy we must admit nothing without proof. Now, as "proof" is very widely used in the sense of "argument," an inexperienced person may be caught in the disastrous fallacy that nothing is to be admitted without being proved by an argument. If this were so, we should never be able to establish the existence of anything, whether of self or of not-self. Be it remembered that proof is the same as evidence; and as evidence is immediate and mediate, so also is proof immediate and mediate. It is not necessary to prove everything by argumentation, by mediate evidence. There is a better because a speedier proof than argumentation, namely, immediate evidence. Immediate certification is of a higher order than mediate certification and should be used when it can be had. Why do we agree to an argument? Because its conclusion is evident to us as seen through the premisses. Why, then, may we not agree to a truth which is evident to us when we perceive it in itself without looking at it through premisses? The absurdity of rejecting certain truths which we can perceive by their immediate evidence only, will appear from the following illustration. With the aid of glasses, single, double, triple, I recognize some object that is beyond the range of unaided vision. My friend who is standing beside me can also with the aid of glasses recognize the same object. But my friend, himself! Is he here beside me? I take the distance glasses, and with them I am unable to see him. He, too, tries the glasses, and with them he cannot see me. Without the glasses we see one another. But because we cannot do so with the glasses which are intended for distance, we agree each to deny the presence of the other. Those who wish to prove everything by means of an argumentation act in this manner. Self-evident truth they will not admit, just because it is self-evident, just because it is so close and apparent that it will not bear the interposition of the medium, of an argument. Every form of scepticism, plenary and partial, is guilty in this particular: it seeks to wedge an argument in between the power and the object, even when the power and the object are separated by nothing more than the geometrical line—which has no breadth; and to wedge it in, forsooth, in order to connect the power with the object.

Evidence is also spoken of as *intrinsic* and as *extrinsic*. It is said to be intrinsic when the truth is perceived or perceivable in itself whether immediately or mediately. Immediate evidence is, therefore, always intrinsic because the connection of subject and predicate in the truth that is immediately evident is perceivable from the known nature of said subject and predicate. The evidence of a conclusion in an argument may also be intrinsic although mediate, for the truth of the conclusion is made manifest in the evidence of what is known regarding the subject and predicate; it is made manifest in the evidence of the premisses, and the premisses are nothing more than the development of the subject and predicate of the conclusion. Now, if the evidence of both premisses be intrinsic, the evidence of the conclusion will likewise be intrinsic, though mediate. What, then, is *extrinsic* evidence? We often hold to truths which are not evident to us in themselves whether immediately or through the medium of a demonstration. We hold to them on account of the evidence of an outside truth which, whilst linking together predicate and subject, still does not put before us the evidence of the bond. This is what happens in our assent to all truths which we accept solely on authority, be the authority divine or human. We have no evidence of these truths in themselves; but we have evidence of the existence of the testimony and evidence of the value of the testimony on the matter in question. Such truths are not evident in themselves. They are evidently credible. The facts of history which we accept, we accept not upon their own evidence, but upon the evidence of their credibility. This is something outside of the connection existing between the subject and predicate of the fact stated, and is called *extrinsic* evidence. We shall devote a special chapter to the value of historical testimony.

94. The Beginnings of Knowledge. In our search for the beginnings and groundwork of knowledge we cannot go beyond evidence and the nature of our knowing faculties which are necessitated to the admission of evidence duly presented.

It may be in place for us to call attention to three primary truths, the recognition of which is implied in every act of knowledge. These three truths are commonly styled the *first fact*, the *first condition*, the *first principle*. They are evident in themselves, and so primary that they cannot be made the subject of a direct demonstration.

The first fact is the fact of the existence of self.

The first condition is that of the possibility of knowledge. The acceptance of this condition is involved in every act of knowledge and lies at the base of human life and action.

The first principle is the "principle of contradiction" which stands guard over certitude in every mental declaration. This principle may be formulated in various ways. Sometimes it is announced as follows: "A thing cannot both be and not be at the same time;" or "The same thing cannot both exist and not exist at the same time." It may be more fully stated thus: "The same cannot be (truthfully) affirmed and denied (cannot be true and false) simultaneously under the same respect." Thus stated, the principle covers the whole range of truths, the concrete and the contingent as well as the abstract and the necessary. The admission of this principle is a necessity to thought. You cannot deny it and hold to your denial. For, if you do, you proclaim the principle, namely, that what you have denied cannot be affirmed.

It would not be easy, nay, it would be impossible to say how these three, the cognizance of the condition, the acceptance of the first fact, the mental grasp of the first principle, follow one another or coälesce in the primitive acts of perception. To understand this we should have to secure a child's account of what happened when it first began to know. We can see—now that we are forced to the admission of the condition by the inevitable impulse of the mind to know—that the first fact always shines with its own unmistakable evidence in every conscious act; and that the first principle is stamped with its application upon every truth according as such truth is known in its contingent or necessary character. This we can see looking back at the distant courses through which our life-thought has cleaved its way; but we are now so far from the starting point to which we shall not return, that the record of the first flight of thought shall never be written in the books of men.

CHAPTER XIV. HUMAN TESTIMONY AND BELIEF.

Some Terms—Witness, Testimony, Belief, Authority—Testimony: Divine and Human; Doctrinal and Historical—Witness: Immediate and Mediate—Belief and Life—Dogmatic Testimony—Sensus Communis—Historical Testimony—Conditions Postulated—Argument in Brief—Contemporary Events—Past Events—Oral Tradition—Writing Monuments—Note.

95. Some Terms. There is a simple fact that plays a marvellous part in the planting and the growth of human knowledge. It is, that man accepts the testimony of man. If all men were to refuse absolutely and in all cases to believe upon the testimony of others, society would be an impossibility. Thus, for the human race, testimony is raised to the dignity of a criterion whereby to pass sentence upon objective truths concerning which those who accept the testimony either cannot or shall not have any immediate experience. The truth is simply believed upon the authority of the witness giving testimony.

A Witness is one who communicates his knowledge.

Testimony is the actual communication of that knowledge.

Belief is the assent given to testimony.

Authority is the sum of motives which the testimony of a witness possesses to urge assent. These motives are, evidence of logical and moral truth on the part of the witness. To believe him we must have evidence of his knowledge and veracity; evidence that he is not deceived himself, nor deceiving us. Thus, we do not believe on the evidence of the truth proposed. We do not perceive its evidence. The truth proposed is the matter, the material object of our faith or belief; but the formal object of our belief, that, namely, which we assent to upon its own evidence, is the knowledge and veracity of the witnesses, whether mediate or immediate. We believe upon the evidence of the credibility of the witnesses. This credibility of the witnesses attached to the objective truth, stands to us extrinsically for the evidence of the truth testified to.

If we consider the nature of the witness, the *witness* will be either God or man; and the testimony will be called, correspondingly, *divine* or *human*. Our *belief*, too, will be distinguished as *divine* or *human* belief, divine or human faith, according as it is founded upon *divine* or *human testimony*.

Divine Testimony is commonly styled revelation. We are not treating here of divine faith through revelation; hence, we merely note the following points in connection therewith:

1. Truths which are outside the scope of the present activity of human reason cannot be known otherwise than by divine revelation. If they could be known by experience, or by intellectual intuition, or by argument, or by human testimony, they would be within the scope of the present activity of human reason. Such truths beyond our natural reach are called mysteries, whether in the broad sense, that they cannot be arrived at by human reason; or in

the strict sense, that even when revealed, they cannot be understood.

2. In regard to certain important truths relating to human life and duty, truths which are, absolutely speaking, within the scope of the natural exercise of reason, it is of value that there should be a revelation,—considering the difficulty, nay the impossibility, of their discovery by each human mind left to its own resources.

Here we leave revelation and take up human testimony. The object of this testimony, the truth testified to, may be doctrinal, as a principle of science proposed for acceptance by belief; or it may be what we call in the strictest sense an historical fact. However, all testimony is, practically, historical. For, even when it proposes to us a principle, it does not present to us the evidence of that principle. If it did, we would accept the principle, not upon authority, but upon its own evidence. So that a philosophical or scientific principle of any kind may be reckoned under the general heading of facts that can be testified to.

Facts are spoken of as

Universal: all physical and metaphysical laws;

Permanent: orignating at some time past, respectably distant, and extending continuously to the present; as, the existence of London;

Transient: not having a continuous or permanent existence, as, the earthquake at Constantinople in 1892;

Periodic: recurring at intervals, whether regularly,

like the return of summer, as the result of the action of physical laws, or otherwise;

Contemporary: happening within the experience of a great part of the men now living;

Recent: The term *recent* takes its signification from the character of the events to which it is applied. A recent fact in the movement of the world's history might be a century distant. The family affairs that served for last winter's gossip in the village are no longer counted as recent.

Remote: The term, remote, is also variable,—events that were simultaneous at a certain time past being regarded as more or less remote, according to the character of the chronicle into which they enter.

The above division is not, nor is it intended to be a logical division. The aim of this chapter is covered fully by the division of the object of testimony and belief into *scientific principles* and *historical events*—taking the word, historical, in its common acceptation. These historical events can be again divided into *present* and *past* events. Present events will include the contemporary. Past events will be *recent* and *remote*.

A witness, as has been said, is one who communicates his knowledge,—one who gives testimony.

A *witness* may be *immediate* or *mediate*. An immediate witness is one who has had personal experience of the fact to which he testifies. Such witness is commonly called an *eye-witness*, since most of the historical facts of which one can have personal experience are those which come under the eye. A mediate witness is one who relates upon the testimony of another. That is to say, he testifies to the testimony of another. A chain of such witnesses may reach down into the distant past, connecting the listener or reader of to-day with the immediate witness and the remote event. Mediate witnesses will thus be either *contemporary* with the remote event, or *quasi-contemporary* (living shortly after it) or *remote* from it; and they will be the more remote in proportion as the event recedes from them into the past and they themselves approach to the present time. Mediate witnesses who have the matter by hearsay are called *auricular* witnesses.

The knowledge of past events may be transmitted by *oral tradition*, by *documents*, by *monuments*.

Oral tradition, or the handing down by word of mouth, implies an uninterrupted series of witnesses beginning with the immediate witness and reaching to the present time. Each mediate witness in the series narrates to a successor what he has received from a predecessor; the immediate witness, of course, gains his knowledge from personal experience. It may be that it is impossible to complete the series so as to bring in the immediate witness,—the nearest connection with the event being its evident unquestioned public notoriety at the time or about the time when it is reported to have taken place.

A Document is any kind of writing which can be advanced as testifying to an event. A document thus becomes the testimony of a witness. When the document is a consecutive record which can be authenticated, it is called history.

Monuments embrace all those more enduring works of human art and industry, the very existence of which leads us necessarily to argue to the reality of certain events with which they must have been connected. Temples, statues, coins, medals, etc., all come under the head of monuments.

96. Belief and Life. There is no one who does not see the great importance, nay, the necessity of human belief in the economy of human life. The human being comes into this world destitute of all experience, and is left during the period of infancy incapable of exercising the power of reason or of making personal investigations. Hence, all those truths the knowledge of which is necessary for the early years of life and which cannot be acquired by reason or experience, must be accepted by the child upon the authority of its elders. The number of these truths, both in the speculative and in the practical order, is very great; and in regard to all of them belief must go before experience and reason.

And even when the days of childhood and youth are gone by and man finds himself in the full vigor of his intellectual power, there will still be many truths, useful and even necessary for the best or the essential conduct of his physical and moral life, of which truths, however, he will never be able to obtain a scientific knowledge, whether on account of the limitations of his genius, the lack of means and opportunity, or the press of duties. These truths he must accept, if he will not fly the circumstances of civilized life, on the testimony of other men in whom he puts his trust. This for scientific truths. And the necessity of accepting them by belief affects not merely the unlearned, but also men of scientific attainments. For, who is there that knows everything about all the sciences? Or who is there that can give the reason for the conclusions which he accepts and acts upon in the affairs of every day life? The crowds that pour out into the streets of the metropolis in the morning, and are hurried from one end of the city to the other on the electric cars, accept with an unhesitating belief that the power which is transporting them is what is called electricity. They know nothing about electricity, nothing about the methods of its generation or distribution or application. They simply associate some external fixtures, whose meaning is a riddle to them, with the general rumor; and the general rumor is based upon the remote declaration of a few whose word has not been called in question. But belief is resorted to not merely by the unlearned. The electrician believes the mathematician, and the mathematician believes the astronomer. The physician believes the lawyer; and the lawyer believes the physician. The speculator believes the telegraph operator; and the philosopher believes the cook. In the higher sciences there is such an interdependence of one upon the other for data, that the expert in the one goes to the expert in the other as the child goes to its mother to have read to it the story which is put up in a wonderful alphabet which it cannot understand. And even in the scientific conclusions that we do arrive at by our own industry, we all know that it is the part of prudence to submit our work to another in whose skill we confide, to have pointed out to us the errors we may have made.

With regard to historical testimony in particular, we may say that belief in it lies at the very base of society. Take away this belief, and the existing structure of civilization will crumble in a night. International relations which rest upon the records of the past will cease, and cannot be renewed. The legal decisions inscribed yesterday will have no value to-morrow. Deeds, mortgages, wills and contracts will be worth no more than the paper on which they are written. All the conclusions of the experimental sciences which are arrived at by induction and repose upon the data gathered during years and centuries, are swept away; and their application in the arts and industries of humanity becomes unfounded experiment. Refuse to believe and you shall not know, when you travel, whether you are in Rome or London or St. Petersburg. The life we have chosen to live is then, we may well say, founded chiefly on belief. Has the belief itself an acceptable foundation?

97. Dogmatic Testimony. Speaking in general, a mere assertion on the part of any person is not sufficient to warrant us in accepting the assertion as true. There may, indeed, be moral truth. The person may be speaking according to his conviction. But we may not have evidence that he himself is not mistaken. This holds very particularly when there is question of scientific doctrine. The mere testimony of a promiscuous one hundred or one thousand persons on a scientific matter may be very well meant at the same time that it is very much mistaken. Thus, the dew is commonly said to fall and it is commonly believed to do so. If, however, one man, well known for his veracity and recognized by the scientific world as a master in his department, makes a positive declaration regarding the matter of his own specialty, it may be very imprudent, even from a practical point of view, to refuse to accept his word. His recognized knowledge, the position he holds in the scientific world, the readiness with which his assertion, if incorrect, would be taken up by other men of skill and reputation equal to or superior to his, put it beyond a reasonable doubt that he would not risk an assertion of the kind without possessing certitude. I do not say that this holds for every assertion of every scientific man of eminence, but only for positive assertions upon matters strictly within the sphere of the specialist. For I know that there is nothing more affected now-a-days by certain writers who are renowned for their experiments upon matter, than the drawing of false conclusions and the making of false assertions outside of their *matter*.

Since, then, we have to read scientific books, and are disposed to accept conclusions within the sphere of the writer, conclusions which we have neither the time nor the capacity to verify by induction or by deduction, it is well for us to know that the credibility of such books may be the more readily recognized

a), in proportion as the subject matter is the more easily studied and hence offers the less occasion for error;

b), in proportion as prejudice is the less liable to enter into the writer's investigation or assertions;

c), in proportion as the writers on the subject in question are the more numerous and the more widely recognized as masters, and have been the more independent of one another in the investigations whereby they have reached the same conclusions.

Hence, we may more readily accept testimony in matters of the direct sciences than in matters of the reflex sciences. The evidence of credibility is much more easily discovered for a work on pure mathematics or on the experimental laws of physics than for a work on ideology or pure metaphysics. You will not hesitate at a book on optics, but you may well pause, to make your selection wisely, when you are looking for a work on the truth of thought. Turn back to our third chapter, the "Chapter of Discord." It may throw light upon what we are saying.

Notwithstanding the influence which the sayings of the wise have upon individual and collective human life, it must be admitted that for the mass of humanity the scientific utterances of the learned afford at best only the strongest kind of probability, and hence can give ground for a very safe opinion, it may be, but not for strictly defined certitude. Still the probability may be so very great as to justify even a prudent man in accepting the utterance as a sufficiently secure basis for action in the material affairs of life. It is sometimes possible, too, with the addition of a little personal experience, to raise this universal consent of the learned upon a scientific conclusion to the dignity of a motive for real certitude. This will depend upon the matter of the science in question. In mathematical science, for instance, which is occupied with algebraic formulæ, one may, after a very limited period of study, come to such knowledge of the character of the science and of the methods of its progress as to see the impossibility of an identical incorrect formula for a given solution being arrived at independently by a thousand skillful mathematicians. The addition of his slight knowledge to the unanimous declaration of the wise will enable him to accept the formula with strict certitude.

To summarize, therefore:

In scientific matters certitude can never be based on the *mere word* of a man.

Great regard, however, must always be had for the authority of the learned, especially when their consent is unanimous.

Still, their unanimous consent cannot justify us in rejecting what reason dictates to us to be evident.

Nevertheless, when reason seems to dictate to us, as evident, a conclusion that is in opposition to the unanimous consent of the learned, it is wise for us to be most willing to reconsider the motives of our assent, remembering that we ourselves may have made an error through haste or prejudice or on account of a narrow intellectual horizon to which we may have condemned ourselves by the limitations of our favorite pursuits.

98. Sensus Communis or Common Consent. In connection with what we have just said comes the query:

what is the value of the *sensus communis*, the common consent of mankind, as a motive for certitude? We have referred to this common consent more than once; and we have seemed to attach much weight to it. The common consent is a testimony. What is its value? What authority has it to command my assent? Its authority, its power to exact the submission of my intellect to the fact testified to, will be in proportion to the evident veracity and knowledge of human kind testifying. Presuming, here, the veracity of mankind, what evidence can we have of the knowledge of mankind? Certainly, there is within us an inclination, established by a long and wide reaching process of induction, to hesitate at rejecting the testimony of the race when there is no evidence of the incorrectness of that testimony. At the same time, we may not forget what has happened, namely, that even during long centuries the human race did accept certain physical, astronomical and geographical statements which the human race now rejects as incorrect. Our question, then, will come to this: is it ever possible for the *sensus communis* to be regarded as infallible? This is never possible if we look upon the common consent *merely* as a testimony. But if we consider the character of certain truths which *are* testified to, accepted, by common consent, the common consent is infallible in their regard. This, however, is not on account of the nature of the universality of the assent, but it is by reason of the nature of these certain truths, the knowledge of which has a direct bearing on the absolute needs of human life, individual, domestic and social. The knowledge of these truths being a necessity to human life, individual and collective, they are perceived in pursuance of a physical law which is just as unfailing as that by reason of which matter gravitates to matter. These truths are what are known as the first and immediate principles and the more immediate consequences deducible from the same. They are truths for the knowledge of which we do not, indeed, require the testimony of the race, since they are all more or less easily discoverable by each one of us; and the immediate first principles always, in fact, present themselves when the time for their application arrives. Still, for the fore-knowledge of such truths, particularly of those immediately consequent upon the first self-evident principles, who does not see that the common consent, as indicated by the uniform action of humanity, is very valuable? For the mind is thus provided in advance with a code of axioms wherein it can find already formulated the solution of a thousand life-problems that arise in the course of a day; and thus the labor of discovery is replaced by the simpler task, the enjoyment, indeed, of verification.

99. Historical Testimony. It is the experience of all of us that we have been able to attain through belief on testimony to true certitude regarding certain historical events. In some instances there was no possibility of immediate personal experience, because the facts were past and transient. There were other instances where personal experience did come later. Yet it did not fortify our certitude: we saw only what we had expected to see. We had the satisfaction of experience: but our certitude would have remained unshaken without it. Again, we have believed: and we have, perhaps, discovered that our belief was bestowed upon an unreliable testimony. With the practical knowledge, then, that historical testimony may be unreliable, why is it that we will sometimes cling to an historical event with the tenacity of certitude when we have nothing to base our certitude upon but testimony which, considered in itself, is capable of leading us astray? The reason is this: circumstances may shed such light upon the testimony as to enable us to secure evidence of its credibility, evidence of the knowledge and veracity of the witnesses.

Putting aside the matter of our own experience, the question we have to investigate, here, is a purely abstract one. We ask: Is there, within the *possibilities*, such a combination of circumstances as *would* warrant us in accepting without hesitation the testimony which witnesses *might* bear to an event past or present? This may seem to be futile as a practical question, when we consider how the severest courts of inquiry that exist in human society send men to their death every day on the testimony of two witnesses, or without witnesses at all and simply on the strength of what seems to be a well woven web of circumstances. But we are not now discussing facts. We are occupied with possibilities. We are not presuming that any such combination as above mentioned has at any time existed, nor that it shall at any time exist. We are not presuming that we have evidence for the credibility of testimony on any one event, be it the existence of St. Sophia's at Constantinople or of St. Peter's at Rome, the fact of the reign of Queen Victoria or of the four years' civil war in the United States. You may hesitate at them all now if you choose. We will ask you to judge for yourself when we shall have closed our investigation. We stop at the possibilities. It is as if we were to ask the question: Is it possible to make the works of a serviceable watch out of aluminum? We have never seen a watch that had aluminum works. But we may arrive at our conclusion by studying the character of a watch and the properties of aluminum. And even if our answer should be affirmative we need not assert that there will ever be a watch with wheels of aluminum.

100. Conditions Postulated. Since we are working in the possibilities, we have the privilege of postulating possible conditions. We shall, therefore, for a trial, postulate the following conditions:

1. The facts shall be such as appeal to the senses. It is of such facts that what we know as history is made up.

2. There shall be persons, one or many as the case may require, who have the normal use of their senses, who are capable of perceiving the fact, and who testify that the fact has in some way, immediately or mediately, appealed to their senses.

3. These persons shall be human beings and hence their actions shall be essentially characterized in the same way as the actions of the men of to-day. We note, particularly, that men act with free will. And

yet we see that, with all their freedom, they do, under given circumstances, pursue certain fixed methods of action, and this with such constancy, uniformity and universality as to leave no doubt that these methods are an outcome of human nature itself. These methods are followed so spontaneously and so unerringly that they are never deviated from unless by reason of some special design. The deviation is thus a noticeable thing, one that attracts attention and naturally incites men to seek for the hidden motive that has been considered proportionate to this deliberate departure from the recognized normal methods. These universal, constant methods have, by some writers, been termed *moral laws*. The term is not aptly selected. For by moral laws we commonly understand the laws that bind the free will of man: the dictates of a superior imposing obligation on the free human will. The moral law, hence, declares what *ought* to be done, the will stfll retaining its physical liberty. Here we are concerned, simply, with what *is* actually and constantly done by the free human will pursuing the tendency of the physical human nature. Now, what are some of the things that our own experience teaches us regarding the uniform and constant methods that man pursues?

We see that man naturally seeks his own good. We see also that man is constantly exercising a natural adaptation which he possesses for the acquisition of knowledge. When he sees that he can reap some positive advantage or escape some misfortune by giving to an event an attention that costs him no labor, he will bestow the slight attention required—

and this all the more readily if the event be of such a nature as to attract attention and to rouse the natural curiosity of the human mind. Even where there is nothing to be gained beyond the satisfaction of his innate thirst for knowledge, he will pause to look upon an unusual deed or object. We see that this inborn love of man for the knowledge of the "facts" (the huge issues of the morning newspapers testify to this craving which calls them into existence) makes him little tolerant of a fellow-man who will belie the facts in a matter in which he takes ever so little interest. Hence, the lie is despised, even apart from its moral aspect. To be known as a liar is to be covered with reproach and opprobrium: whereas, one of the first titles to esteem is to be of tried repute for truthfulness. Thus it comes to pass that men in their various relations with one another seek for the fair fame of the truth teller and shun the stigma that is put upon the liar. Whence it follows that men form a habit of truthfulness, which becomes a second nature. A lie is not told deliberately unless there be some personal satisfaction to be obtained by the lie together with the strong probability that the lie will not be discovered, or, that, if it be discovered, the personal advantage hoped from it will—according to the depraved estimate—be considered sufficient compensation for the inconvenience of being branded as a liar. Hence the old saying that, no man is a liar *gratis*, but that when he does falsify deliberately there is a strong motive behind the falsification: avarice, ambition, fear, revenge or some such passion.

Finally, whenever there arises a false rumor concerning a matter in which the public is interested, the rumor is always promptly contradicted; and the contradiction comes all the sooner if there be persons to whom the rumor may prove inconvenient or hurtful.

It will be noticed, as we have stated before, that we have not spoken of the deep moral motives underlying the conduct of men. We have been occupied in considering uniform results—so uniform, indeed, that they must be regarded as the outcome of native forces in humanity. It has not been our intention to specify all those forces. But, so far as the constancy, and uniformity of results goes for the establishing of the conclusions which we have just called attention to, each one of us has, in his own personal experience with mankind, collected data more numerous and more exhaustive than the data that have ever been demanded for the formulation of any law in physical science.

Such, then, shall be the human beings whom we shall suppose to be the witnesses testifying.

101. The Argument in Brief. We can now briefly propose the argument for the possible evidence of credibility in historical testimony:

It will be possible for historical testimony to possess evidences of credibility, if it be possible for it to be accompanied by circumstances or conditions which evidence the knowledge and veracity of the witnesses. But it is possible for historical testimony to be accompanied by such circumstances or conditions. Therefore it is possible for historical testimony to possess evidence of credibility.

The *minor* of this argument, namely, that it is possible for testimony to be accompanied by such circumstances, is made plain from a consideration of the conditions postulated above. We take a case in which testimony is rendered on a notable fact that is obvious to the senses; we assume that there is a sufficient number of witnesses having the normal use of their senses; and we choose an event of such a character as to preclude the possibility of collusion on the part of the witnesses. Now: each one of the conditions or circumstances is possible in itself. No one of the conditions is incompatible with the co-existence of any other one condition or with the co-existence of all the other conditions. There is nothing repugnant, therefore, in their simultaneous existence as accompanying testimony at the present time or at any other time. Therefore it is possible for testimony to be given under circumstances that will lend to it the unmistakable evidence of credibility, so that we may establish ourselves in certitude regarding the event testified to.

It may be useful for us to indicate the manner of applying these principles to the knowledge of events both contemporary and past.

102. Contemporary Events. According to the general principle, certitude concerning contemporary events can be based on testimony when we have evidence of the credibility of the testimony; and we have evidence of this credibility when we have evidence of the knowledge of the witnesses and evidence of their veracity.

It is possible for us to have evidence of their knowledge. We shall select a fact that is very obvious to their senses, even if their senses be a little obtuse. Let the fact be an earthquake, an eclipse, a holiday parade, or a great storm at sea. If the witnesses be many, and unanimous in their testimony, we cannot doubt of the fitness of their senses for the perception of the fact. A general and uniform illusion or hallucination in such a matter would be a physical impossibility, particularly if, as we may suppose, the event should have been foretold by exact science, or should leave after it marks that lie open to the investigation of the rest of men. We have chosen a sensible fact which forces itself into notice, which takes the attention captive, which is public and simultaneous to all, and which demands no scientific knowledge for its observation. And, if necessary, we may presume that there are present in our great crowd of witnesses some who are capable of making a scientific note of the event, and whose testimony agrees. Hence it is possible to have a case in which we can have evidence of the knowledge of the witnesses.

Now, for their veracity. We choose a possibility: a public fact, declared by many who,—though differing in tastes, pursuits, years, religion, habits, nationality, education, prejudices,—agree, nevertheless, in their testimony. Considering the various interests here involved, a lie that could go undetected would be an utter impossibilty. We are supposing men to be what we know them to be; and—to make our argument available for any time—we have no right to suppose men ever to have been anything else. The circumstances have been so selected that the same motive to deceive could not have affected all the witnesses. The lie that would have brought momentary glory to one would have brought immediate and perpetual shame to another. Whilst it might have been to some a means to future enjoyment, it would have been to many only the price of suffering which they could not be supposed thus to court, in conspiracy, for pure love of the lie. And, in order to have evidence of their veracity it will not be necessary to introduce all the varieties of conditions mentioned above. It will be fully sufficient to have even but one condition which would so affect the witnesses as to render the lie an impossibility.

Nor will it always be necessary to have a multitude of witnesses. A few persons testifying to a fact that can, when known, turn only to their own detriment, carry the evidence of their own veracity. Thus, if three men testify to a murder which they committed in cold blood, there is nothing in the nature of things which does not evidence the credibility of their testimony. Again, if a few witnesses give testimony to a fact in which others are deeply concerned and which these others have both a solemn interest in refuting and the ready means to refute, but which they accept and acknowledge; this very acceptance gives to the testimony of the few the element it requires for the evidence of its credibility. Remember, that I am here speaking for the scientific, and not for the mob.

There are many falsehoods, religious and political, which are thrown out to be swallowed by the mob, which does not examine. The refutation of these falsehoods has been given over and over again. But the mob always exists, and good men, who will not be heard by the mob, have to bear with the opprobrium that is ever cast upon them by envy and jealousy and the revengeful pride of humbled ambition.

The force of testimony will be all the more readily recognized when those who give it have no earthly advantage to expect from the giving of it, but rather contempt, annoyance, persecution, torture, and even death. If we might refer to a case in point we would instance the testimony of the apostles.

Recalling what we said (Nos. 51, 52) about objective truths of the metaphysical, physical and moral order, we might ask the question: to which order does the credibility-of-testimony, as an objective truth, belong? When the testimony is evidently credible, do we hold the connection between the testimony and its credibility to be metaphysically, or only physically, or only morally necessary? We said (n. 51) that any individual fact of which we have immediate personal evidence, presents itself with evidence of its metaphysical necessity. For being so, it is absolutely impossible that it should simultaneously and under the same respect, not be so. But in the matter now under consideration we have not immediate evidence of the event. We know it no otherwise than through the credibility of witnesses. To what order of truth does this credibility belong? Does the credibility evidence itself objectively as a metaphysical, as a physical, or as a moral necessity? Testimony, in itself and merely as testimony, does not carry with itself any evidence of its credibility. It is only when it is allied with certain conditions, as presented above, that there can be any evidence of its credibility. But when the testimony is fortified by these conditions, does it present itself as something with which credibility is evidently joined in metaphysical, physical or moral necessity? To this we reply that the necessity of connection between testimony and credibility may be found to be sometimes of one order and sometimes of another. This will depend upon the combination and the accumulation of the conditions. We may see that the testimony is credible and at the same time recognize that the witnesses retain the physical power of giving false testimony: there will here be moral necessity, but not physical. Again the case may have been examined with such minuteness and the consequences of the testimony may be such, that there is absolutely no good to be derived from a falsehood. Now we know that the will never acts except in view of some good. Hence a falsehood under the circumstances would imply such movement of the will as is excluded by the physical nature of the will. It would be equivalent to non-gravitation on the part of matter. The necessity of connection between the testimony and credibility would be a physical connection. It would have to be admitted as we admit any law in the physical universe. Finally if the fact is testified to as one that is public, patent, standing; if it is testified to by the whole human race, by individual travellers and by entire peoples in the affairs that concern their national life; if it be a fact, for instance, such as the existence of a place called France,—we come so close upon the border of a metaphysical necessity in the junction of credibility with the testimony that there is no longer any distinguishing a difference, if difference there be.

We suppose, of course, that you have never gone out to look for a place called France. But many of your friends tell you that they have been there; and they have brought you presents from Paris. You have written letters to friends who were said to be in France, and these letters reached them. You have seen great ships—each one of them worth a vast fortune—lying at the docks of Boston, New York, Philadelphia, Baltimore and New Orleans; you have seen them come and go, disappear and reappear out upon the bosom of the ocean at the rim of the horizon, with the regularity of the departure and arrival of the suburban trains of your own city. You have seen your friends, who professed to be going to France, take passage on these ships; and you have seen them return on the same. You have read of the French Empire and of the French Republic as institutions of your own time. You have read of the deeds of the French in the Crimean war, of the downfall of Napoleon the Third, of the death of President Carnot. You have seen Ambassadors of France at Washington, and French Consuls in every large city that you have visited. I might continue to accumulate testimonies until you should be forced either to admit that there was a place called France or to suspect that the whole human race had leagued in one grand conspiracy whose sole and ultimate end was to make you believe a falsehood; a falsehood, however, for the immediate correction of which by personal investigation, every means was being put at your disposal by the entire membership of the vast conspiracy. Is the conspiracy possible? Consider how few persons you know; and how few know you. In view of this, can you suppose that the human race should be devoting its time, energy and material resources to the work of making you believe a geographical mis-statement? The supposition involves the most perfectly concealed collusion throughout the entire organization of human society in all its departments, civil, social, military, industrial, commercial, international. The fortunes of the world are involved in the lie; and millions of human beings are uncomplainingly wearing out their lives in abetting it. And all the conspirators know full well that you will need but a hundred dollars and two weeks of vacation to bring their enormous deceit to a very shameful end. Now, to come to the point, what is the necessity of connection, in this case, between the testimony and its credibility? Does there, in this case, remain any possibility whatever of the testimony not being credible? Does the objective truth, *this testimony is credible*, present itself to you as a metaphysical truth, that is, as evidencing, under the circumstances, absolute inseparability of the predicate from the subject? If you do not choose to call it metaphysical, you must at least allow the connection between subject and predicate to be so close and necessary that you would not feel justified in hesitating at the testimony unless you knew that the mental condition of all men, yourself alone excepted, was out of the normal.

103. Past Events. We have established the possibility of certitude regarding contemporaneous events. Is it possible that we should be able to affirm with certitude the past reality of an event said to have taken place a thousand or two thousand years ago? May we affirm with certitude the past existence of a Roman Empire, and of a Roman Emperor named Augustus? The case is the same as if we were to ask: Is such a combination of circumstances possible that in the year 3000 it might be affirmed with certitude that there existed a British Empire in the nineteenth century? Could the present fact be so transmitted that there might be evidence of credibility in the testimony that related it? We are taking a fact of such a nature that there can be no doubt about the credibility of the contemporary testimony. But could this testimony go down from age to age accompanied by its credibility? Let us suppose that the British Empire should cease to be this very day. Suppose that Great Britain and Ireland should have sunk into the sea last night. There would still remain the English language; there would remain the histories of England, written in all the languages of the earth; and there would remain the official records of all the nations of the globe. But suppose that all these histories and all these documents should be burned this night and that the English-speaking peoples should wake up to-morrow morning speaking another language, German, or French or Spanish, and that the English language should in the slumber of a night become not only a dead language but forgotten. There would still be vast multitudes of peoples who would have lived in or visited England; and their testimony would be credible. Then we shall suppose that all those who had ever seen England shall die to-night. Now, what about to-morrow? There is not an eye-witness left. You see, we are taking circumstances that involve far greater difficulty for the transmission of the event than is involved by the circumstances of an event that transpired a thousand years ago, but in connection with which we still have the same people, the same language, the records of the time, the same unchanged face of nature, the hills and valleys and rivers that the record tells of, and even the towns or cities—if not in preservation, at least in ruin—whose streets and monuments have stood as silent witnesses and have been visited and written about by every generation from various climes through the lapse of a thousand years. But in the case we are taking, we are supposing that to-morrow morning there shall not be an eye-witness left, not a vestige of, nor a written word of reference to the past reality of Great Britain and Ireland. And just as you are convinced to-day of the existence of France, so would you be convinced to-morrow and next month of the past reality of Great Britain and Ireland. Your conviction would be the conviction of the human race. The disappearance of Great Britain would be immediately recorded in history. The learned men of the day and the officers of the various governments of the earth would vie with one another in trying to commit to writing all that they could call to mind of the story of the lost island. Would the next generation be able to form an undoubting judgment regarding the past existence of the two islands? Would the credibility of the testimony of the men of to-day be evident? The next generation would admit the fact without a dissenting voice, as the men of to-day admit it without a dissenting voice, as the human race contemporary with the fact admitted it without a dissenting voice. If, then, the testimony of the present generation possesses evidence of credibility for the next generation, the testimony of the two generations will possess the evidence of credibility to force the assent of the third; and the testimony of three generations will possess the evidence of credibility to force the assent of the fourth generation. And so the evidence of credibility will perpetuate itself in such a way that it will force the assent of the men who shall live in the year 3000. And this can happen, too, even if the testimony be transmitted only by word of mouth, by oral tradition. This should suffice to show us the possibility of affirming a past fact with certitude.

In conclusion we shall add, that when an event has been handed down through long ages, without any denial worthy of serious consideration, this single circumstance of the unbroken length of testimony is a plea for acceptance which may not be overlooked.

The general question being thus determined, we shall, now, make a brief reference to the means by which the knowledge of past facts is handed down. These means we may classify as oral tradition, writing and monuments.

104. Oral Tradition. Where a distant fact has been handed down by oral tradition, a condition of the reliability of the testimony will be, that the fact itself be one of a very notable and public character, one which would naturally attract the attention of a great many persons. It will be necessary, moreover, that there be no break in the chain of testimony reaching down from the fact to the present time. Besides, at each new stage in the progress of time, the body of mediate witnesses will have to be sufficiently large to warrant us in admitting that they had evidence of the credibility of the testimony of those who preceded them. And it must be remembered that in regard to the substance of a notable fact it is not easy for a general error to creep in, since there are three generations living at the same time; and if it were possible for parents universally to give the same incorrect information to their children, the error would be corrected by the grand parents still living. Amongst rude tribes who have no written record, the credibility of a tradition is the more worthy to be considered, in proportion as it is found to be the more generally cherished by the whole people, the wiser heads as well as the simple; and the credibility of a tradition will be still more deserving of notice if the substance of the fact be found to be preserved independently amongst different peoples.

105. Writing. In order that documents, or writing, attesting a past fact, may possess for us the evidence of credibility, we must have evidence of their authenticity, of their substantial integrity and of their veracity. By authenticity we mean that the writing is the work of the author to whom it is ascribed; or, if the writer's name is not given, that it was written at the time at which it is said to have been written.

The authenticity of a work is to be judged of upon both intrinsic and extrinsic evidence, that is, both from the internal characteristics of the work and from the traditional recognition that has been accorded to it. Some of the necessary internal marks are to be found in the language, the period written about, the personal character exhibited in the writing and the opinions set forth. The turns of speech must certainly not be of later origin than the age to which the book is to be accredited; nor should they belong distinctively to a previous age, unless there is evidence that the style is an imitation of the style of that age. The persons, facts, customs, etc., must not be of a date later than that claimed for the execution of the writing. The tastes and character of the actual writer as shown forth in the book must not be in opposition to the well known tastes and character of the alleged writer. We could hardly be asked now to admit in good faith that a low comic chronicle just discovered should be set down as the work of Cicero or of St. Augustine. So, too, if the book, in treating of grave matters, contains opinions that are clearly contradictory to the known opinions of the writer as expressed in authenticated writings, we cannot admit the contradictory work unless we have clear evidence that the writer changed his opinions.

Amongst the exterior signs the most significant is an uninterrupted oral or written tradition regarding the authenticity of the work. This mark will be all the more effective in evidencing the authenticity if we find the tradition holding firm under the futile attempts of hostile critics to discredit the authenticity of the work. The only case which we have of such permanency under bitter, hostile attacks, is that which illumines the authenticity of the sacred writings of the Hebrews and the Christians.

By integrity we mean completeness. Absolute integrity demands absolute completeness—no mutilation and no interpolation. Substantial integrity in an historical composition implies merely that there be no substantial change from the primitive texts. Supposing the primitive texts to be authentic, a book written later upon the same subject without substantial change will be reliable as to the substance of the facts.

But, with all this, it will still be necessary to pass sentence upon the veracity of the writing, upon the knowledge and truthfulness of the writer. To do this we must go back and judge the writer as we judged of those giving oral testimony. If the event be one of public importance and the writer be an eye-witness or an auricular witness amongst those the credibility of whose testimony we recognized above, or if his account be made up from authentic public documents and monuments, and if, moreover, no contradiction of his statement has existed in writing or in oral tradition, we cannot safely doubt his veracity. And thus it may come to pass that a single historian may supply us with plentiful motives of credibility. This will be the case if he be a public man of recognized good judgment and erudition in his day: if he wrote of his own times, and his writings were then accepted as correct; and particularly if the substance of what he narrates has been carried down by oral tradition through two or three generations and his work has been kept and referred to as the true statement.

106. Monuments. Monuments may be relied upon when they relate to a grave, public event and are known to have been fashioned at the time of the event to commemorate it—no one venturing to contradict the event or the significance of the commemoration. Should such monuments be discovered to have been constructed long after the time of the fact they are intended to commemorate, they are to be held merely as the opinion of the time at which they were constructed; and this opinion will have to be passed upon under the light of history and oral tradition.

107. Note. In this chapter we have not pretended to discuss the canons of historical criticism. Such discussion would by itself fill a respectable volume. We have wished solely to uphold the possibility of arriving at true thought on the evidence of the credibility of testimony. Thus we have not felt it necessary to refer to certain principles which may serve for the rejection of a narrative, principles which may regard the nature of the events put down, or the capacity of the witnesses as compared with the nature of the events, or the literary methods of the writer. Neither, again, has it entered into our scope to expound the laws which must be applied in the balancing of probabilities or in the making of a choice when confronted by opposing testimonies.

CHAPTER XV. CONCLUSION.

Summary of Method—The two Extremes and the Middle—What is Evident?—A Quiet Process—Sensus Communis.

108. Summary of Method. In the first and second chapters of this book we endeavored to state the problem that is involved in every act of judgment, in every mental conviction: Is the judgment true? Is there an object corresponding to the mental assertion?

In the third chapter we emphasized the difficulty by presenting the conflicting replies volunteered by a number of writers. The selection of writers was made with the view of exhibiting every shade of assertion and denial in opposition to the common-sense verdict of humanity.

For the purpose of avoiding long refutations we tried to find something which all these writers necessarily admitted and upon which we ourselves were necessarily at harmony with all of them. We found our point of agreement in the affirmation of self. In this affirmation we had the recognition of the first fact, self; the acceptance of the first condition necessary for the pursuit of knowledge, namely, the admission of the possibility of knowledge; the recognition of the first principle without which not even the affirmation of self can be sustained, the principle of contradiction which saves us from denying simultaneously what we affirm.

In seeking for the reason why self is affirmed with conviction we found the sole and universal reason to be, that self presents itself to be known, provided with an indubitable testimony to its existence, that is to say, provided with an *evidence* that cannot be gainsaid. Upon this evidence we affirm the existence of thought as our own; and of pleasure, pain, feelings and emotions as belonging to self.

Upon the very same grounds universally recognized as absolutely necessary and fully sufficient for the affirmation of the reality of self, we affirm the reality of the world of not-self, the reality of the object of each knowing-power. The life of cognition, then, is never a mere seeming to be. It is a veritable knowledge of truth which is objective independently of the cognition. As we affirm self, so do we as inevitabfy affirm the existence of body-belonging-to-self; the existence of matter or body which is not in any way identified with self; and the truth of certain principles or laws which govern the activity of self and of not-self. All these things come before us with an evidence as strong as that whereby we are forced to recognize the existence of thought and of the self to which it belongs. Hence, if we admit the reality of our thought and of our self, we must admit the reality of all the rest upon an equally valid testimony, which is its own evidence. By sight and double contact we take in the evidence of the existence and conformation of our own bodies. By all the external senses we are put into communication with an external world and receive its evidence. We shall not come to know all about this external world. But, what matter?

Neither do we know all about thought, nor about anything else that is identified with self. We have not a thoroughly comprehensive knowledge of any object that comes under our observation, be it intellect, thought, self, matter or the qualities of matter. But this is no reason why we should deny the existence of any one of them, or of so much of their nature as may be presented by evidence to even the untutored perception. And evidence unfolds itself and knowledge grows with observation, study, association and instruction.

109. The Two Extremes and the Middle. The idealist, engrossed in the study of thought and of the intellectual ego, fails to give credit to the evidence brought to him through the external senses and treats the material world as though it were as immaterial as his idea of it. He denies, in fact, the certified reality of an outside world of matter, saying that he has no means of getting beyond the fact of his own impressions, that is, beyond the knowledge of the modifications of the conscious ego. Yet, he will admit your existence and mine. Indeed he writes books for us. He admits that each of us is a conscious ego. Now, he can know of the existence of conscious intellectual egos other than himself only after having become aware of the existence of bodies identified with these conscious egos; and he can know of the existence of such bodies in no other way than through the action of his external senses. But accepting the testimony of the senses for the existence of the bodies of other men, he must, if he will be consistent, accept the same testimony for the reality of the whole external world.

The materialist, on the other hand, is engrossed in the study of matter, in the observation of the material phenomena that present their evidence through the senses. And so much account does he make of this evidence which the idealist denies, that he assumes sensible observation to be the sole test of reality. In other words, he assumes that matter alone exists. Of course he cannot ignore the fact of thought. Hence, to be true to his assumption that matter alone exists, he has next to assume that thought is but a movement of matter, perhaps a vibration of the brain. Thus, as the effort of the idealist is to explain his sensible perception on the basis of pure thought; so the effort of the materialist is to explain pure thought on the basis of sensible perception, or even to reduce all perception to mere vibratory movement of matter.

We admit the evidence that both of them admit. But we avoid their ungrounded assumptions at the start; and we reject their false conclusions at the close. We follow the guidance of nature, which is always consistent. Materialist and idealist, each, from his opposition stand-point, practically repudiates one half of nature because it will not fit his theory. Each constructs a theory from his own opposite half-view of the case, and then fits the theory to the rest of the case. But how? By assuming the rest of the facts to be what they are not: by assuming them to be what they would have to be for the welfare of the preconceived theory. We are told that there is thus an advance towards scientific unity. But that is a very costly unity which is purchased at the price of ignoring the facts in the case. It is not scientific. It is not knowledge. It never rises above hypothesis: and even as hypothesis it is worthless, because it is based upon an unwarranted assumption.

Unity is admirable: so is variety. But bare unity is monotony: bare variety is confusion. We do not neglect either one. We unify the varieties of intellect and sense, of thought and sense-perception, in the pervading identity of each conscious, complex self.

110. What is Evident? We have evidence then,

Of self and its various modifications, thoughts, volitions, and of a body belonging to self;

Of bodily organs that receive impressions from an external world;

Of that external world which contains other conscious egos like unto ourselves;

Of truths which, as general laws, pervade the working of nature.

We have evidence, too, that this, our varied capacity for receiving evidence, works, if I may use the expression, automatically. Putting the evidence and its due presentation to the normal faculty, the result is inevitable and follows by a law as precise as the laws of movement and gravitation which regulate the changes and conserve the equilibrium of the solar system. We can no more fail to receive evidence of whatsoever kind, duly presented to the normal faculty, than the paper thrown into the fire can fail to burn or than the elastic ball striking against the hard surface can fail to rebound. The susceptibility of the conscious ego to the action of evidence, and the conscious recognition of evident truth, are as unerring, according to the varying degree of conditions present, as is the execution of any law in the physical universe. In saying this I do not wish to exclude the influence of education and of personal liberty. For, these will condition both the general habitual readiness of receptivity and the momentary act of perception. Education develops the receptivity. By education (including all that it implies, observation, instruction, etc.) evidences are accumulated, combined, co-ordinated, submitted to the processes of synthesis and analysis of induction and deduction. Thus it will come to pass that truths which to the uneducated are utterly imperceptible, certain causes, effects, relations, similitudes, contrasts, may stand out in evidence before the educated mind whose receptivity has been developed by that which it has received. On the other hand, as we have seen in the chapter on error, passion, free will and preoccupation can divert the attention and thus prevent an evidence from being, as it would otherwise be, fully and duly received. Moreover, the physical condition of the sense-organ may be such that admission is denied to the entire evidence which is necessarily admitted by an organ in the normal state. One person may be color-blind; another may be deaf. Yet each one receives according to his receptive condition; no more, no less. If either one errs, his error does not affect the physical law of receptivity. The sense responds with an exactness that is strictly proportioned to its abnormal condition.

111. A Quiet Process. It is to be noted that in the perceiving act the work gone through by the faculty or organism is not itself perceived. The perception goes straight to the object known. No one can fail to see that, in the process of cognition, this is a wise ordination. The cognition goes on rapidly and undisturbed. In the same manner, when the will commands according to the cognition, the powers are set moving in silent harmony—the intermediate processes between the pure volition and the final act willed following one another mysteriously towards the execution of the final objective purposes.

You go about, day after day, thinking, acting. You form new concepts, ideas, notions, new judgments, new trains of reasoning. You resolve to act out the conclusions of your mental argument. Your attention is engrossed by the facts and principles which are the objects of your thought. The work done is exclusively subjective, and yet the direction of your attention is as exclusively objective: so quiet and rapid is the pace of thought, and so silent and unperceived is the presentation to the will of knowledge that is to be acted upon. Long practice under the gentle tutorship of nature has taught us the swift and easy execution of many a mental feat whose processes will ever elude the labored, albeit keen, scrutiny of the closest student of psychology. The lessons of nature are learned without being adverted to: they are less tedious, more expeditious, more unerring than any we find in the schools. It is only when we hesitate at the value of a judgment formed regarding objective truth, that we try to form *explicitly* the other judgment, that *we know that we know.* And even then, this second judgment is not formed by a study of the first, but by a renewed study of the object in whose evidence we expect to certify or discredit the prior mental act.

112. Sensus Communis. We have insisted throughout upon the *sensus communis*, the common sense, the universal, uniform, constant consent of mankind upon the objective value of thought. Not that we make this common sense the criterion, the ultimate reason for any affirmation; but we have to recognize in it the natural and necessary effect of the real criterion which is evidence.

There exists and there has, beyond denial, existed uniform and universal amongst men, an invincible conviction regarding the trustworthiness of the faculties and regarding the objective value of thought and sense-perception. If we should seek to apply to the conviction the test of experiment, we should find that in each individual the conviction would be supported by a series of experiments more extensive in range, more varied, more exact, more numerous, than those that have served for the formulation of any law—of any thousand laws—in physical science. And we should find that in the case of each individual these experiments began so early and were so unremittingly carried on by the force of the conditions of human existence, that the conclusion made itself felt as an essential condition of life even before the young mind was capable of the act of reflection or of explicitly making a scientific induction out of its untold experiences. Any theory, then, of human thought and existence which will not stand the test of the inevitable conditions of humanity must be rejected by one who would be recognized as being in the normal state. Every philosophy that breaks away from the fundamental laws of human existence becomes upon the instant only the hypothetical fiction of an individual mind fancying to itself what would be if things were not as they are.

The recognition of the objective value of thought is the basis upon which the practical life of the human race has been founded from the beginning. The failure to recognize it must necessarily make life a practical impossibility.

We know that what we have said throughout this work is an unreserved condemnation of that mixture of doubts, denials, inconsistencies and contradictories, which has been labeled "modern philosophy." A philosophy that antagonizes the universal, elementary convictions of the human race which are primarily essential to the existence of the race, is not the philosophy for man. And thus primarily essential is the universal conviction regarding the truth of thought. Dispense with it, and there is an end to the thought itself. It is necessary everywhere, in private and in public life. It is as necessary to the continuance of the human family as primary movement is to the conservation of the solar and sidereal universe. Take away this primary movement, and you will have a crash of worlds that will fill space once more with vapor and atomic dust. So take away man's necessary conviction as to the truth of thought, and in sixty days earth will become a great cemetery covered with the remains of the entire human family, left there a prey to the beasts of the forest which will soon have made their lairs where kings just sat on thrones.

So the final philosophy of the truth of thought is, that it is the law of man's nature and that he must abide by it.

ALPHABETICAL INDEX.

Numbers refer to pages.

Milton Keynes UK
Ingram Content Group UK Ltd.
UKHW010636030424
440506UK00010B/1284

9 781014 473929